Advance Praise 1

Jim Autry's poems have long snatched my breath by the beautiful and impressive ways they reveal the life of the man—his good heart, his keen eye, his feeling for the experience of others. They are full of surprise and delight at common things made marvelous. Read them slowly, read them aloud, read them with others. Prepare to laugh and cry, to pause and reflect, and to feel immense gratitude for moments of illumination and ecstasy, longing and remembrance. Jim Autry writes for thinking hearts.

—Bill Moyers

I've been reading and re-reading Jim Autry's poems for over thirty years. They still make me laugh, cry, wonder, and rejoice. I'm grateful for his voice in the world.

—Betty Sue Flowers
Editor, *Joseph Campbell and the Power of Myth*
Former director, Johnson Presidential Library

I was privileged to publish James Autry's first two books of verse: *Nights Under a Tin Roof* and *Life After Mississippi*. In his hands poetry is about first love, baptism under fire, lessons learned, rain on a tin roof. At an abandoned farmhouse, the family long gone, daffodils keep coming up every spring. His voice is one of patience and staying power, and we are the better for it.

—Lawrence Wells
Publisher, Yoknapatawpha Press

ON PAYING ATTENTION

 **PEAKE ROAD**

Peake Road Press
6316 Peake Road
Macon, Georgia 31210-3960
1-800-747-3016
©2015 by James A. Autry
All rights reserved.

Library of Congress Cataloging-in-Publication Data

Autry, James A.
[Poems. Selections]
On paying attention : new and selected poems / by James A. Autry.
pages cm
ISBN 978-0-9915744-3-8 (pbk. : alk. paper)
I. Title.
PS3551.U879A6 2015
811'.54--dc23
2015001911

ON
PAYING
ATTENTION

New and Selected Poems

JAMES A. AUTRY

Also by James A. Autry

Books

Choosing Gratitude 365 Days a Year: Your Daily Guide to Grateful Living (with Sally Pederson)

Choosing Gratitude: Learning to Love the Life You Have

Looking Around for God: The Oddly Reverent Observations of an Unconventional Christian

The Book of Hard Choices (with Peter Roy)

The Servant Leader: How to Build a Creative Team, Develop Great Morale, and Improve Bottom Line Performance

The Spirit of Retirement

Real Power: Business Lessons from the Tao Te Ching (with Stephen Mitchell)

Confessions of an Accidental Businessman

Life & Work: A Manager's Search for Meaning

Love and Profit: The Art of Caring Leadership

Poetry

Nights under a Tin Roof: Recollections of a Southern Boyhood

Life after Mississippi

Videos

Love and Profit

Life & Work

The Spirit of Work
(Available from StarThrower,
800-242-3220 or www.starthrower.com)

For my wife Sally Pederson,
Friend, Lover, and Partner
in all the glad and sad tidings
of our thirty-two-year (so far) marriage.
Words will never be enough
to express my gratitude.

Acknowledgments

I must begin with Larry Wells, owner of Yoknapatawpha Press in Oxford, Mississippi, who took a chance on me and published my first and second books of poetry which, incidentally, are the first books included in this collection.

Next I thank Betty Sue Flowers who mentored me in poetry over three decades, giving me both critique and confidence.

I am blessed that many friends have let me subject them to readings of these works over the years. There are too many friends, alas, to list but prominent among them are those who for thirty-two years have gathered for a Columbus Day weekend in Vermont and have had a profound influence on my life and work.

I am also very grateful for the people at Smyth & Helwys, especially publisher Keith Gammons, plus I have been very fortunate to have sharp-eyed, creative, and efficient Leslie Andres as editor.

Finally, I thank my family, two of whom, wife Sally Pederson and son Jim, have poems in this book. Thanks to both of you.

And thank you, readers, for your appreciation of poetry.

Contents

From *Life after Mississippi* (1989)

From *Love and Profit* (1991)

From *Life & Work* (1994)

Introduction

by Curtis Wilkie

At intervals during a remarkable lifetime begun with the experience of growing up in the rural South before becoming an Air Force fighter pilot, a journalist, a romantic, an executive of a magazine empire, twice a husband, and father of an autistic child—Jim Autry has committed many of his thoughts to verse.

He appreciates the value of words, knowing he must be economical, using the boldest ones in his vocabulary to express himself in a limited number of lines. Laid out in simple, stark rows on the page, his words sparkle like gems on a strand.

In his newest collection, *On Paying Attention*, Autry's poetry sings of boyhood intrigues in mystically Protestant Mississippi where "our fear of shame was stronger than our fear of snakes." He tells of other fears, of flirting with doom in unfriendly skies; of pain and joy and sadness and love and death. In Autry's words, cold business decisions that confront the spectre of failure or the loss of jobs turn into lyrical accounts of life on the bottom line.

Autry was reared in a land where "they yelled about babies born and people cured / about fires and broken bones and cows loose and dogs lost," where funeral congregations were consoled by a choir that "brings a balm in Gilead / and a roll is called up yonder." His early recollections are interspersed with voices from his childhood, admonishing him: "Mind grabbing those scraps like that boys / good way to lose a finger."

We follow him as he matures, as he grooves to saxophone riffs by street musicians in Manhattan, as he makes love in New Orleans to "the raw sounds of Bourbon Street / a background for her moans and screams." He gives up bohemia for the world of business; he is successful, but all is not happiness. Firing a salesman is "like a little murder / taking his life . . . ." There is a poignant a retirement party where "they come and talk / about how he will be missed, most of them never noticing he was there." Even while taxiing safely at the end of a commercial flight at O'Hare, Autry is reminded of danger: "That fear born of something much older than airplanes / rises like a siren in your brain."

In his sixth decade, as his second wife Sally gives birth, he wants the assurance of a healthy baby: "I count toes and fingers / and check his little penis…and watch the doctor probe and squeeze / not believing everything came out all right."

Through years split by splendor and apprehension, he perseveres.

Now eighty-two and afflicted with the beginning of Parkinson's, Autry acknowledges mortality: "My life has been around a while / but, I can tell, is thinking about / moving on and taking me along . . . All I can do is drag my feet / finding reason after reason not to go."

If *On Paying Attention* is a valedictory, it is a grand closing statement.

Curtis Wilkie *teaches journalism at the University of Mississippi and is the author of* Assassins, Eccentrics, Politicians, and Other Persons of Interest, *the latest of his four books.*

Preface

I wrote my first poem when I was a freshman in college. (Readers will be relieved to know that it is not included in this book.) Though I made my living as a journalist for many years, I did not write another poem until 1976 when, during a period of personal difficulty, I heard James Dickey reading his poetry. I went home from that and, after a glass or so of wine, wrote six perfectly awful poems. (They also are not included in this book.)

I began to write poetry regularly at that point, seeking critique and advice from people whose work I admired. Principal among those was Betty Sue Flowers, who was not only a most important mentor but also became a dear friend to my family and me.

One evening in Oxford, Mississippi, the late Willie Morris and I did a program on magazine editing at the University of Mississippi, where he was a writer in residence. Afterward, he led a group of students and me to his home where he read from his book, *Terrains of the Heart.* Then he turned to me and said (or commanded), "Read something, Autry." All I had in my briefcase were some poems about my boyhood in Mississippi. I read those, and Willie said, "Come home, Autry, and publish." He mentioned me to Larry Wells, owner of the Yoknapatawpha Press, who then read what I'd written and said, "If you can do a book of these, I'll publish them."

Those poems became *Nights Under a Tin Roof: Recollections of a Southern Boyhood,* the first of my books, most but not all of which include poetry.

I have chosen to begin this book with those Mississippi poems, then continue chronologically with selections from each book, ending finally with a collection of new, unpublished poetry.

I hope that something here will touch your own story. Whether that happens or not, let me hear from you. I'm on Facebook (Jim Autry), and my e-mail address is JAutrydsm@aol.com.

—Jim Autry, January 2015

From
*Nights Under
A Tin Roof:
Recollections of a
Southern Boyhood*
(1983)

Nights Under a Tin Roof

I

When the fire still sends its yellow light from the bank of coals
is best
before the cold pushes us under the quilts
while the frost is still invisible in the air
And we can look up to the uneven planks fifteen years from the
    sawmill
and still not painted
and make things and faces in the wood grain
and be scared and laugh

> *You boys settle down in there*
> *We'll be getting up 'round here*
> *in a few minutes*

But we wouldn't
as we didn't stop peeking the cracks at Allie Jo and Mae Beth

> *You see Allie Jo's pants*
> *You didn't neither*
> *Did too when she blew the lamp*

Peeking those same cracks that let the wasps through
that always needed stuffing with paper.

Uncle Virgil covered the kitchen cracks with wallpaper from the
catalogue but mice ate the wheat paste making tunnels like moles
and Uncle Vee mashed them with his fist and pulled them through
so the kitchen wall had little holes in the printed roses where a tunnel
stopped
And the rest of the rolls are wrapped in newspaper under the bed
because it might work better someday with another paste

Now you boys don't pee off the porch
do your business under the chinaberry tree

Those same cracks that let the smells through the floor
like the time Aunt Callie put out the ant poison and the rats got it on
their feet then licked them and died under the house

You ain't smelled stink till you smelled
an old wolf rat dead with the poison

And who had to rake them out with a stick
who was little enough to squeeze under the floor scared of snakes
and gagging with the smell

Take 'em yonder to the gulley boys
mind that lye on your hands

II

When the rain plays different notes
high near the peak and low in the middle
is best
When the thunder is far off down the Tippah bottom
and the wind is settled to breezes
and early before light we hear the back door and Uncle Vee's boots
and the pine fire in the stove and the lid on the salt box
and the pot boiling

Boys don't put so much sugar
in that coffee

But there was always the lightning when it struck the cat
right out of Jimmie Lee's arms and burned out the screen door
and killed the cat and only knocked Jimmie Lee down

Thank you Lord for that sign

And we can't go out in it especially under the trees
or go near the stove or windows

    Stay on the bed and don't touch the floor boys
    and don't bounce

and only the girls can use the slop jar except when it lightnings
and we always need it then

    Well use the slop jar boys
    but you'll have to take it out

When the dark comes with the afternoon clouds
and we hear lightning striking the pines on hickory nut hill
and the air whispers like God shushing everybody before the thunder
we try not to jump when it comes
and Aunt Callie brings tea cakes from the kitchen
round and sugary and crumbly with burned bottoms
and chewy with thick middles
and cow's milk to dip them

    Don't drip on the quilt boys

And Uncle Vee crumbles cornbread in blue john milk
and rocks and looks out the window

    It'll be dry 'nough to pick up potaters boys
    if the lightnin' didn't scare the life
    outta preacher mule

III

When a whip-poor-will sets in the yard and calls another in the garden
is best
and we sleep on top of the covers
when the windows are propped open
and balls of last year's cotton are wired on the screens with hair pins
keeping out the flies

And we hear Uncle Vee hiking there the Walker hounds
to the bottom below the old place

> *Just listen at the window boys*
> *you'll hear the hounds good as me*

And Aunt Callie washes a block of ice from the sawdust pile
and puts it in a pitcher of cistern water

> *Don't play around that cistern boys*
> *we'll never see you again*

That's when the snakes come out
like the copperhead that bit Aunt Callie getting up the cows
and Uncle Vee tore his shirt for her heel
and we ran all the way to Cousin Verdell's who had a Dodge

> *Knowed somethin' was wrong boys*
> *when I heard your feet slappin' the ground*

When the night doesn't cool down
Uncle Vee puts his feet in a dishpan of water
and Miss Ann fans with the big palm leaf James Edward brought from
Hawaii before he got killed on the destroyer in the Solomons
after Becky won the Miss *USS Edward Turner* contest
and his dog Frisco just went off and died

Let him go boys
he don't want you to find him

Uncle Vee doesn't sell the place
but he'll let me put a house on it someday
with a tin roof

Best roof in the world if you nail it right boys
take a twister

And it keeps the place dry
and turns away the summer sun
and sends back the fireplace heat through the winter cracks
And holds everything together through the storms

Communication

Now we dial the phone
but Aunt Callie still yells into it
and ends every sentence with a question mark
as if she can't believe that all her words
can get through those little wires

But back then we stepped out and pointed our voices
across the hills

    Whooooeeee

It would follow the bottoms and up the next hill
and in a few minutes
it would come back from Cousin Lester

    Whooooeeee

When there was trouble
Uncle Vee would blow the fox horn
or ring the dinnerbell
and someone with a car would come
not knowing the problem but that we needed a car.

When Uncle Vee yelled or blew the horn
there was a message to send

    Don't you boys be out there
    yellin' up somebody
    'less you got somethin' they need to know

But we'd yell
and the old folks would know we were just yelling

and let it go
our high voices somehow falling short of the next hill
the dogs not even coming from under the porch.

Weeks would pass without a real yell
Then it would roll up the hill from Cousin Lester's

    Whooooooeeeeee

And Uncle Vee would stomp out on the porch
and cup his hands and answer
and turn his head and listen
nodding at the message I could never understand.

It's how we heard Cousin Lottie got snake bit
and James Louis came back from the Pacific.

It's how the fox hunts were arranged
and the hog killings set

They yelled about babies born and people cured
about fires and broken bones and cows loose and dogs lost
the words always short and spaced
for the distance they had to travel.

Now there are the wires
but Aunt Callie still yells for the distance
and looks at the phone
holding it so her eyes can aim the words
through the instrument and across the hills
where they are to go

Cotton Poison

We called it cotton poison
and its smell became good
drifting across the roads with the dust
lying in clouds on the July fields
Because underneath
we knew it was killing the weevil
and the weevil had killed us
every year before

Until the poison came
the cotton was armpit high and good
but inside the weevil was doing his work
Until the poison came
we carried barlow knives to the fields
and mashed the weevil from the split boll
hoping one hard death would scare the others
and heal the cotton
Until the poison came
it was God's will and the weevil was his

Now the poison drifts with the tractor dust
and the soldiers come home from Okinawa and the Bulge
ride into the night and jump in the river
the dust floating from their overalls
and laugh themselves dry
thinking of a bale to the acre
Because they beat the weevil like they beat the Nazis and Japs
and all their daddies could do was pray

The Snakes

There were snakes
my god there were bad snakes
but we didn't see all that many
except in Aunt Callie's imagination
under every log and in every brushpile

> *Now you chirren watch*
> *you'll step on a snake*

We knew them all
the copperhead/rattlesnake pilot/highland moccasin
(all the same snake)
plus the gentleman rattlesnake
who would always rattle before he struck
and the treacherous cottonmouth
hidden beside the path waiting for the chance to bite not run

> *Cottonmouths got to discharge that poison*
> *so they got to bite somethin' or somebody*

And there were copperbellies not poison but mean
and after Uncle Vee killed them
he pushed their heads into the soft mud with a stick
deep so half the snake was in the hole

> *It's a sign our family*
> *killed the snake*

And there were good snakes especially the king snakes

> *You ought to see him kill a bad 'un boys*
> *wrap hisself around that other'n*

and squeeze him to death

But we killed them all
because a snake was a snake

Well I couldn't tell, Uncle Vee
they all look bad

There were spreading adders that puffed and hissed and acted mean
but couldn't hurt you
and rat snakes and bull snakes and hog nose snakes
and chicken snakes that ate our eggs and baby chicks
and when you reached into a nest on a high shelf in the chicken house
an old settin' hen might peck you
or it could be a chicken snake
so sometimes eggs in a high nest would go rotten
because we'd all think the next day's cousin would get them.

There were blue racers and black racers
and one time rabbit hunting
Uncle Vee and Cousin Lester saw a racer and kicked it
like when they were boys
and it curled up in a ball
and the other one kicked it high in the trees
it staying in a tight little ball
then both running for it and Cousin Lester kicking Uncle Vee
and they both falling in the leaves

Won't that kill the racer, Uncle Vee?
Sure will

And glass snakes that broke into pieces when you hit them
yes, really into sections
each one wiggling on its own

On Paying Attention

You leave him alone boys
he'll get back together
no matter how far you scatter them pieces
take one a mile away he'll get back together

One day on the path to the spring
Jimmy Lee and I saw a hog nose snake swallowing a toad
so we watched him do it
throwing his jaw all out of joint
the toad kicking his legs and hopping
making the snake's head jump off the ground
like a snake with hind legs in its head
then when the toad was inside
we killed the snake and cut him open
and the toad hopped away.

But the mean snakes were moccasins
even the un-poison ones
the brown water snakes at the swimming hole
that come toward you with open mouths hissing

They got a nest here somewhere boys

and we always argued whether they could bite you under water
and we never found out.

After Aunt Callie got bit by the copperhead
all the men went hunting for bad snakes
with hoes and some shotguns
They turned over logs and whistled at brushpiles
saying a long straight whistle will bring them out
and at the end had killed hundreds of snakes
bad and good
and we measured the longest ones
and some of the boys skinned them for belts.

From *Nights Under a Tin Roof: Recollections of a Southern Boyhood*   13

Then we didn't worry about snakes for a while
and hoped maybe they were all killed off

> *They'll be back boys*
> *they were in the Garden of Eden*
> *and they'll be back here.*

Seasons Came with Food

I

Seasons came with food
not the other way around
certainly not with rain or winds or sun
or any weather at all
But when onion sets and potato cuts went in
it was February and the red sand soil
was cold under the fingernails
and our noses ran

Now you chirrun
keep those coats buttoned

Then it was mustard greens
we sowed in patches
to mix with wild poke salad
or collards that would take the frost.

When the water warmed we'd fish
for lazy willow cats hungry after the winter
or blues or jugheads or the quick channels
caught on set hooks and trot lines
run late at night in a boat
or barefoot along the slick bank
fighting mosquitos and scared of cottonmouths

Don't step over a log
you can't see the other side of, boys

Girls picked dewberries low on the ground
and somebody would make a pie

I declare you chirrun
eat yourself sick
if I let you

Aunt Callie would can the rest
sweating over the steaming pots
with summer almost here
and the garden in and the greens up

> *A mess of greens and a pone of bread*
> *won't be long now*

Then it seemed something all the time
squash and new potatoes and green onions
the meals getting good and the canning hotter.

II

There came the day when
we soaked rags in coal oil
and tied them on our wrists and ankles

> *Them chiggers love blackberry bushes*
> *better'n I love blackberries*

And we'd fill our one gallon buckets
with the dark berries staining our hands
and chiggers getting past the coal oil
with the wasps nests and the yellow jackets
and always the snakes

> *Copperheads love to lie up*
> *in the shade of those blackberries*
> *so make plenty of noise chirrun*

On Paying Attention

Then everything was easier
with only some wild plums to pick
and potatoes turned over by a plow
looking rich and good in the dirt
and stored in piles in a dark place
under the house

> *Now don't you boys whine about spiders*
> *just mind your business and come back*
> *for another load.*

We ate peas and corn and tomatoes and
greens and onions and cornbread
and drank buttermilk
when the cows got into bitterweed
and the sweet milk tasted bad
And when everybody was full of watermelon
Aunt Callie made preserves from the rinds
and ground and chopped squash and cucumbers
and pickled little hot peppers
to pour over the greens and sop with bread.

III

By September the woods smelled of muscadines
and we picked them by the gallon
shaking trees and laughing when they rained on us
then finding them among the leaves

> *I declare you chirrun eat more*
> *than you put in the bucket*

Their seed sacks shot into our mouths
as we sucked the musky hulls

And Aunt Callie canned some and made jelly
and preserves and acid drink

Now I tell you that ain't wine
and I don't want to hear no more about it

and if we were good
fried pies crisp outside
where they almost burned in the skillet
and sometimes skim cream
to put on a cobbler
we'd eat in front of a young fall fire

You spoil those chirrun to death

And we'd clean our guns
and talk about deer and rabbits and ducks and quail
and laugh at who'd miss
and who'd have to clean the rabbits

Worse smell
Lord I'd rather skin a skunk

Or Uncle Vee would get the smokehouse
ready for the hog killing

IV

Still later when ice was on the ponds
with the salt box full
and jars on the shelves
the colors of their contents tempting us
the comfort of it would settle upon us
and some morning soon after Christmas

before a pine fire
Uncle Vee would be looking out the window

> *Think we'll put the potaters*
> *between the fruit trees this year boys*
> *might's well use that ground*

then one day it wouldn't seem so cold
and we'd hear the gee and haw
and the chains on the single tree
and the soft tearing of the new ground
over the plow

Buzzards

I

Buzzards would stack
a hundred at a time
the highest fly specks in a hot summer sky
and circle something dead
And we'd wonder what it was
and talk about walking to it
through the woods
sighting on the stack of buzzards
until we'd arrive underneath
and there it would be
whatever it was
Dead and big
we knew it would be big

II

But we did it one time
making two buzzards fly
filling the air
with their awful smell
and it was only a rabbit
all those buzzards for one dead rabbit
Were they waiting their turn
up there a mile
turning turning never flapping a wing
not a feather
riding on some wind we couldn't see or feel
and waiting a turn
on one dead rabbit?

On Paying Attention

III

It was the depression maybe
no money and no dead things
A lot of buzzards
with not much to do
We would watch them for hours
Sometimes instead of chopping cotton
Stopping in the field
Leaning on a hoe
Lying by the big cedar

Things Done Right

I

Now there are ruts in the floor
where Aunt Callie rocks with a morning cup of coffee
and warms her feet at a gas heater
whose black pipe shoots into the old chimney
where the fireplace had been.

But back when the ruts were young
the first sounds of morning were ashes being stirred
the thump of fresh logs
the pop of pine kindling in the cook stove
the quiet talk of the grownups
and the radio with its thin and fuzzy hillbilly music

> *How many biscuits can you eat*
> *this mornin' this mornin'*
> *How many biscuits can you eat*
> *this evenin' this evenin'*
> *How many biscuits can you eat*
> *Pillsbury biscuits can't be beat*
> *this mornin' this evenin' right now*

and the weather reports Uncle Vee always turned up.
We'd hear him walk to the door
and know he was looking at the sky

> *Don't care what the weather man says*
> *gonna rain this afternoon*

Then the radio would go down
and Aunt Callie and Uncle Vee would have their quiet time
and talk about the day

and he would say where he planned to work
and she would talk about washing or canning
or sewing or working the garden
and they would decide what we children would do
We'd hear the hiss of something frying
and wonder what it was before we could smell it
salt meat or bacon or maybe country ham

> *Better call those chirrun*
> *biscuits goin' in*

And the smells settling into the whole house
all the way under the covers
would help us wake up

II

Even in the hot of July
the cook stove was fired
and Aunt Callie baked biscuits every meal
using her big wooden dough bowl of flour
and pinching in lard and squeezing in buttermilk
working it only with her hands
then lifting the dough and rolling it out
cutting the biscuits with a baking powder can.

And there might be fried pies
sealed with a fork dipped in water
and pressed evenly along a crescent edge
Or a fruit pie with a tall crust
scalloped by the quick and perfect twists
of a buttered thumb and forefinger
Between meals Aunt Callie kept the stove hot
simmering a slow pot of string beans and salt meat
boiling water for dishes

heating irons on the day after wash day
How she would sweat in her loose wash dress
ironing everything from the clothesline
sprinkling with her hand dripping from a pan of water
sometimes pressing a cedar cutting under cloth
to make a pair of church trousers smell better
working fast before her iron cooled down
licking her finger and sizzling it against the iron
to check its hotness
as it sat on an old coffee can lid
at the end of the ironing board
And leaving no piece of cloth untouched
dish towels, sheets, tablecloths and wash rags
overalls and work shirts
which would be sweat wet and wrinkled in five minutes
even undershorts
and always making us boys change everything every day

> *What if you's to be taken to the clinic*
> *or somethin'*
> *you want to be dirty?*

And folding everything on shelves and in drawers
as if they would never be touched
but be looked at and admired
and passed on
by some work clothes inspector.

On other days she churned
humming hymns to the wet rhythm of the dasher
the kitchen filled with bowls and buckets of milk
clabber or blue john or buttermilk
with cheesecloth keeping out the flies

III

And Uncle Vee was the same
the way he hitched his mule
and plowed his garden
geeing and hawing up and down the rows
always in the same direction
The way he put in his potatoes and onion sets
then unhitched the mule and fed and watered him
The way he measured two double handfuls of shorts
for each hog and mixed it with slop from the table
as if the hogs might not eat it done wrong
And in the evening after supper
laid a fire with pine knots and split wood
so it burned with one match
and never had to be stoked a second time
then sat with a cup of coffee
and always worked on something
maybe patching a stew pan with screws and a washer
or rigging a trotline or cleaning his double barrel
or sharpening his barlow knife
spitting on a whetrock
and drawing the blade toward him and away
and testing its sharpness against the hairs on his arm

>*Most dangerous thing in the world, boys*
>*is a dull knife*
>*cut you faster'n a sharp one*

and while Aunt Callie snapped peas or shelled butterbeans
he would peel an apple
putting his barlow to it and turning the apple
so the peel came in one long spiral
stretching halfway to the floor

You ain't peeled an apple
till you can do that, boys

And when we tried it
then and much, much later
the peel always broke and fell
and the apple never tasted the same

Scenes of Courtship

I

They said she was an old crazy girl
who lived at the bottom of the hill
and we always honked when we went by
thinking of all the things we'd do with her
if only we had the nerve to stop

> *Blow the whistle Junior*
> *then step on it*

And we'd honk at any time of night
stepping on it before her father
could get to the window

> *He tole the sheriff*
> *he was gonna shoot anybody who honked*

On Saturdays when the crop was laid by
we'd put on khakis and a white shirt
hitched up two turns on the sleeve
our arms white above the sun browned hands
and we'd cock our elbows out the window
looking over our shoulders
sucking a match stick toothpick
and make the square slowly
but still spinning the tires on the turns
the white '46 Ford pickup washed with buckets from the creek
a white wall tire on the tailgate
and a skull turning knob on the steering wheel
And we'd go to the dance at the national guard armory
and listen to Jimmy Deal and his Rhythm Ranchers
and sip moonshine from fruit jars in paper sacks

and get brave enough to dance with country girls
because we thought they were easy
in their flour sack dresses
and their legs scratched from shaving with their daddy's razor

Now we gotta go straight home
after the dance

But we'd head for the moonlit cemetery
four in the pickup seat and always squeezing closer
when shadows moved among the stones

Start the motor
I know I saw somethin' that time

And our hands would fall in laps
and be pushed away
or our fingers would brush as if by accident
the soft bosom front of those flowered dresses
our khakis tightening with the intensity of that touch

I got my hand right on it Junior

II

But that was so much later
Than when we courted at revival meetings
fanning through the singing and the preaching
every morning and every night
swimming in the afternoons
driving there in Winston's courting car
the '37 Chevy truck with the cab cut off
open to the dust and gravel
taking a load to the creek and going back for more
jumping from the bank of the little Tobi Tubbi

On Paying Attention

named for an indian chief's wife
and the coldest creek in the country

> *Hey Winston dive on down*
> *and bring us up some ice*

And the girls would wear shorts over their bathing suits
some with the new elastic suits in light colors
and others in the old wool suits
that would get loose and sag open at the leg.
Someone would bring a watermelon from the creek
where it had been cooling
and we'd squirt the seeds from between our thumb and forefinger
until we were spotted
then jump in the Tobi Tubbi and wash them away

> *Y'all better come on, we're going to be late for revival*

III

When the big boys went off to the war
and came home in their uniforms
we'd hide in the bushes where they parked
and watch them press their girls against the car seat
or sometimes in the summer
lean them backwards against the fender

> *He put his hand*
> *up her sweater Junior*

while we only played spin the bottle
at birthday parties
and didn't press against anyone
and didn't have uniforms

IV

It was a sin for a Baptist to dance
so we went with Methodist girls
who taught us to slow dance and jitterbug

> *Hey look at old Junior*
> *do the dirty boogie*

Until one time
when Betty Sue Wilford fell off the bridge
and broke her arm and got scratched up
and Ben Edwin had to carry her to Oxford in the coupe
and the old people found out about the dancing
and made us pray for forgiveness
and Ben Edwin couldn't get the coupe anymore

V

But later when Junior bought the pickup from his daddy
and fixed it up
we had four in the front seat every Saturday night
and parked at the cemetery
and sometimes one couple would get back in the bed
on some hay and an old quilt Junior kept in a tool box
the girls always afraid the other was watching

> *If they can see us*
> *Marianne will tell everybody in school*

Until one night after a dance at the Water Valley armory
when I couldn't go
Junior and Betty Vee Fox hit ice on the Tallahatchee bridge
And all we could do was put black borders
around their pictures in the yearbook
where Junior was handsomest and Betty Vee was wittiest

VI

Then everybody graduated and got jobs
or went to the army
and there was a lot of marrying
And those who went to college
came back every once in a while
but didn't want country girls anymore
and would not be seen in a pickup truck

Grave Digger

His name is Otis Cox
and the graves he digs with a spade are acts of love.
The red clay holds like concrete
still he makes it give up a place
for rich caskets and poor
working with sweat and sand
in the springing tightness of his hair
saying that machine digging
don't seem right if you know
the dead person.
His pauses are slow as the digging
a foot always on the shovel.
Shaking a sad and wet face
drying his sorrow with a dust orange white handkerchief
he delivers a eulogy

Miz Ruth always gimme a dipper of water

Then among quail calls and blackeyed susans
Otis Cox shapes with grunt and sweat and shovel
a perfect work
a mystical place
a last connection with the living hand

Cousin Verdell on Food

When I eat those drumsticks from some chicken
who never scratched the dirt
I think of Cousin Verdell's ideas about food

> *Best thing to eat*
> *is somethin' that'll eat*
> *somethin' else's droppin's*

And the thought of it made our mouths taste bad
and we figured Verdell was crazy

> *I tell you boys*
> *you think about it*

But we didn't want to
so we'd talk about fishing
and he'd talk about catfish

> *They eat dead stuff off the bottom*
> *I seen 'em eat manure*
> *and they absolutely the best tastin' fish*

Or we'd say we had to do chores
and he'd talk about pigs

> *Eat any damn thing*
> *eat they young'uns*
> *eat snakes*
> *eat all kinda slop*
> *and they absolutely the best meat*

There was no stopping him
until after the chickens

> *And chickens*
> *Boys they foller*
> *other animals 'round*
> *just to eat the corn outta they shit*
> *Hell they eat they own shit*
> *And what'd you rather eat than fried chicken?*

Verdell said God gave all those things a special organ
a purifying system
a way of taking what other creatures wasted
and turning it into something good.

But he wouldn't know what to say now
about a chicken who never scratched the dirt

The Outhouse

I

It happens in places where they fold toilet paper
in little points
Where the seat is contoured
and the flush handle is from the modern museum
Where the tub is pastel
and the towels hang on heated bars
Where the sunlamps are on timers
and magnifying mirrors scissor out
to show the back of your head
That I think of all the terrors of the outhouse
on a dark and cold night
with wind bending the pines
with screech owls
with dogs howling in the bottom
and who knows what waiting
in that dark and putrid cavern below the splintery seat
maybe a new and unknown something
hatched from that awful murk
lying there or sliding or worming its way upward
waiting for that next soft bottom
to block its only view.
Or even things known and feared

> One time an old boy over'n Union county
> got bit right on the dingus
> by a black widder. Died.

II

We'd play so long and hard at the end of a day
we never wanted to stop

Now if you boys have to do a job
you better do it before dark

But sometimes we wouldn't
or we'd time it all wrong
or it would hit us after supper.
And how could the grownups tell?

You better go on out there now
you can't wait till mornin'

They always knew
and we couldn't undress for bed
until we took the coal oil lantern
and some pages from the catalog or newspaper
and after trying to get someone to come with us
just to stand outside
and after calling the dogs
who also seemed to know it was a wasted trip
whistled our way down the path
and into the shadowy drafty spidery three holer
talking loudly to no one
kicking the floor and seat
trying sometimes to squat balanced above the hole
so our bare skin would not be exposed to whatever there was
and finally
did our job (as Aunt Callie would say)
and made our way back
toward the lamp lit windows of the house

Crow Killer

Why did he want to kill the crows
when he could talk to them
and call them up
and when they made him so happy
fighting owls and coming to his voice
when he created out of his own mouth
a battle
a mortal struggle
setting them against their old enemies?

But he killed them in a dozen clever ways
with cow bell around his neck
and an old brown patchwork quilt over his back
crawling
on all fours among the cows
mocking their rhythm
swinging his head
ringing the bell
moving slowly toward the big beech tree
where the crows perched outsmarting everybody in the county
except Mr. C. W. the crow killer
who rose up from under the patchwork
with his double barrel
and got two
their awkward black bodies falling among the real cows
who hardly jumped when Mr. C. W. pulled the triggers.

But his favorite was the fight
the old owl crow fight
which started in his throat
and went out across the bottoms

caw caw caw
who-who
who-whoo

whoooooo
whooooooo

Sending the message
that a bunch of crows had found an owl
had disturbed his daytime sleep
had set up upon him
and were diving dodging driving
the old enemy from his resting place.
It was more than crows could resist
and they came to the sound
looking for the battle
eager to claim a piece of the kill
but Mr. C. W. was the killer
stepping from his hiding place
still cawing and hooting
right up until he pulled the triggers
always dropping two
black among the green leaves.

One time he almost missed
and a crow fell with a broken wing
and he took it home
and put it in his henhouse
with a splint on its wing
and fed it and trained it
to sit on his hand.
Then he took it to the woods and let it caw
while he hooted
a Judas crow
calling its friends and family

On Paying Attention

to die two at a time
one from each barrel.

One time I asked him why
and he said they eat corn in the field
and that seemed reason enough
but he fed his Judas crow corn from the crib
And when the crow died
old Mr. C. W. didn't come around much
but we would see him at the store
stocking up on shotgun shells
or hear him cawing and hooting
down in the woods
calling in crows
and killing them two at a time.

Fox Hunt

Is it true the fox loves the hunt
and plays games with the pack
while men squat around fires
and boys stand back and slap mosquitos
or sleep on a car seat
or on the shelf of a coupe
or in a pickup
and wait for the chase?

> *Hike there! Speak to 'em!*
> *Speak to 'em!*

And do the dogs know they should not catch him
but just bark
and try to get ahead of the others

> *Old Peaches is moving up, Lester*
> *about in the middle*

and let their masters know
so they can talk about it
and spit in the fire and laugh at the sound
and teach the boys to love a dog's mouth
and know it as it comes out of the bottoms
through the pines?

> *Old Phoebe has kindly of a yodel,*
> *don't she*
> *a real pretty mouth*

And do the men think on the mystery of it
for boys bred hunters

to run to the crossing place
sucking the wet night air
pointing the flashlight and not a gun
for the shining of that red and white tail

> *Go to ground any time he wants to*
> *but he don't look tired yet*

Then light another fire and listen
as it settles on them
how foxes and other things
move easily through dark woods
leading their chase and going to ground
only at their pleasure?

The Copperhead according to Mother Ruth

(for her grandchildren)

Get him with a hoe
but don't step on the head

He'll bite you
even dead

Remember Aunt Callie
between heel and tree
he bit and ran
from Uncle Vee

Look in brushpiles
circle them wide
he's their color
and he'll hide

He's God's creature
but it's also true
you must do unto him
before he does unto you

Christmas

I

We always talked about white Christmases
but there rarely was one.
They were mostly gray and wet and cold
that cut through our mackinaws
when we went for the tree
Preacher mule pulling the sled
down through the pasture and across a cotton field
with some unpicked still hanging ragged white on the stalks
to the bottom of cane and honeysuckle and sawbriars
and a few patches of cedar or pines.
We'd look at every tree

> *We could cut the top*
> *out of a big'un, Uncle Vee*

Then we'd tie it to the sled
and Preacher would pull it up the hill
his breath smoking from his nostrils
some of us running ahead
to tell the coming of the best Christmas tree

II

In the kitchen Allie Jo and Aunt Callie popped corn
from a little patch Uncle Vee planted every year
on the edge of a feed corn field
(and sometimes the August sun was so hot
it would pop on the cob)
and strung it on sewing thread
coiling it on the table
like a snake of popcorn

And we'd try a handful
complaining at the taste

> *We didn't put any salt on it*
> *'less you boys eat it all*
> *'fore we get it strung*

Uncle Vee mounted the tree on some scrap boards
and set it upright in a corner
across the room away from the fireplace

> *One spark boys*
> *and the whole house'd go*

When the popcorn snake was wrapped in and around the tree
we tied ribbons on the branches
and hung last year's Christmas cards
Aunt Callie had saved
most with a manger scene
or a picture of stained glass windows
(which we would see only years later
in city churches
where the people had money
and the preachers thought stained glass was important).
Sometimes we stuck cotton balls in the tree
and one year Aunt Callie tried making snow
from Ivory Snow like in a magazine
but it dried and crumbled on the floor
and Uncle Vee said it was more mess than it was worth.
We blew balloons and tied them like colored balls
and when the pine needles popped them
we would suck the rubber pieces
into little balloons in our mouths
then twist and tie them
making the tree shabby with colored rags of rubber

III

Cousin Hamer had a crystal radio with earphones
because he was blind from when one of his brothers
hit him in the eye with a sweet gum ball

The boys was meaner'n house dogs
but they didn't mean any harm

and we took turns listening to Christmas carols
from big churches off somewhere
probably Memphis.
He would tune and tune the radio
and pass the earphones around
until the batteries got weak
and the music sounded farther and farther away
Then we'd sing for him
and have a prayer
and go home
always blowing out the lamps before we left
because he didn't need the light

IV

We got a few pieces of candy at Christmas
chocolate covered creams shaped like upside-down cones
and hard peppermints
and tangerines
like oranges that were easy to peel
Stockings
big boot socks full of tangerines
and pecans and jawbreakers and sometimes a grapefruit.
Uncle Vee always saved the biggest ham in the smokehouse
salt cured and smoked and two years hanging
and Aunt Callie would soak it and simmer it all day

then chill it in the coldest corner of the bedroom
farthest from the fireplace
and Uncle Vee would sharpen the butcher knife
until we'd be scared to touch it
and slice the ham so thin we could almost see through it

Mind grabbing those scraps like that boys
good way to lose a finger

We put the ham in biscuits
not fat dough biscuits but thin crusty ones
baked special for Christmas.
The rest of the food was the same as any Sunday
only there was more of it
maybe three kinds of meat
and more cakes and pies and teacakes
and we got to eat between meals

V

Morning was always early but Christmas was extra early
the first up stoking the fire and getting in wood
not complaining of the cold floor or the early chores.
Santa would have eaten his teacakes and drunk his coffee
and left us clothes mostly
a belt or gloves or rubber boots
or flowered shirts and dresses
from feed sack patterns we had seen in the feed shed
but never questioned that reindeer feed
must also come in printed sacks.
One year there was a mold for lead soldiers
and a little melting pot and a bar of lead

Now you got to be extra careful
with that hot lead boys

And we made the same soldiers
and killed them in battle
and melted them down
and made them again
until we burned out the mold

VI

Everybody acted happier
except when we prayed that all the soldier boys
would be home from the war by next Christmas.
We went to church and sang carols
and sometimes acted out the baby Jesus story
using old sheets and robes to be wise men and shepherds.
And the preacher said
wouldn't it be nice if we could keep
the spirit of Christmas all year long?
And we thought it would be nice
and told ourselves we'd try

Misplaced Woodsman

I see a woodsman in the parking lot
stopping amidst the cars
as if he did not have to stop
studying the stars
as if he did not know his direction now
smelling the air
as if seeking the wetness of a yonder river.

The woodsman's mind moves easily through the trees
barefoot across the slick bottom
bending poles and snapping sawbriars
leading the lost fishermen
out of the river
out of the storm.

I see a woodsman in the parking lot
turning at the car
as if waving the hunters ahead
bracing on the door
as if mounting a flat bed pickup
pressing and twisting
as if he needed no new legs.

The woodsman's mind cuts himself from under the fallen tree
hefting the McCullough with a sure hand
lifting limb by limb
making finally a crutch
complaining later that he should have stayed
until the job was done.

I see a woodsman in the parking lot
leaning as if there were no rubber tip cane

shading his eyes as if the pigeons
were a string of high geese
cupping his ear
as if expecting sudden wingbeats
or the bays of a far-off pack.

The woodsman's mind hears one voice among the hounds
figuring where the pack will cross
laughing at the red and white tail
sleeping later like the fox
the chase over
calmly gone to ground.

I see a woodsman in the parking lot
watching the sky for darkening clouds
as if no dams had stopped the floods
as if there were no beans where the water had been
measuring the horizon
as if the safe route were his to choose
as if no highways cut through the ancient hills
as if there were no air conditioned cab
no four wheel drive
no CB radio
As if there were none of those things to make life easy
without a woodsman.

Progress

I

In the browning picture the whole town sits
man woman and child
smiling from the stump
workmen with axes and saws to the side.
How had it looked
a cypress big as a town's population
and tall as Poff Hill
its round top knees like children wading
all lamps and coffee tables now
and it confined as pecky paneling?

II

In the black dawn where the big trees had been
we waded mud for a mile
to the flat bottom boat
another mile on the water and we were not yet to the river
or beyond to the deep slash
of the duck, beaver, muskrat, egret, snake
their place gone now to beans
waist high across the bottomland
making forty bushels on an acre of memories

III

Boiling okra slimey stews and singing in Ira's pasture
Cajuns channeled the Tippah and drained the old run
their big machines ripping the willows and straightening the bends
bringing land where the flood was
pushing out the cottonmouths and beaver dams
pushing out the bream the sweet willow catfish

pushing out the mysteries of the deep slash
proving it was mud and water after all.

Genealogy

You are
in these hills
who you were and who you will become
and not just who you are

> *She was a McKinstry*
> *and his mother was a Smith*

And the listeners nod
at what the combination will produce
those generations to come
of thievery or honesty
of heathens or Christians
of slovenly men or working

> *'Course her mother was a Sprayberry*

And the new name rises
to the shaking of heads
the tightening of lips
the widening of eyes

> *And his daddy's mother was a McIlhenney*

Oh god a McIlhenney
and silence prays for the unborn children
those little McKinstry Smith Sprayberry McIlhenneys

> *Her daddy was no count and her daddy's daddy was no count*

Older brother Jim Goff said it
when Mary Allen was pregnant

> *Might's well send that chile*
> *to the penitentiary soons he's born*
> *gonna end up there anyway*

But that lineage could also forgive
with benign expectation
of transgressions to come

> *'Course, what do you expect*
> *his granddaddy was a Wilkins*

or

> *The Whitsells are a little crazy*
> *but they generally don't beat up nobody outside the family*

or

> *You can't expect much work out of a Latham*
> *but they won't steal from you*

In other times and other places
there are new families and new names

> *He's ex P&G*
> *out of Benton and Bowles*
> *and was brand management with Colgate*

And listeners sip Dewar's and soda or puff New True Lights
and know how people will do things
they are expected to do
New fathers spring up and new sons and grandsons
always in jeopardy of leaving the family

> *Watch young Dillard*
> *if he can work for Burton he's golden*
> *but he could be out tomorrow*

And new marriages are bartered for old-fashioned reasons

If you want a direct marketing guy
get a headhunter after someone at Time Inc.

Through it all
communities new and old watch and judge and make sure
the names are in order
and everyone understands

Off Again
(Reflections of the Modern Traveler)

Off again
in all directions
like a chicken with his head cut off
like a blind dog in a meat packing house
like all those things
the old people would say
if they could see me now.

It was the same
plowing a mule geeing and hawing
in the hot wet sun
sweating a spot on the porch
at dinnertime
then off again
to the slanting red fields.

It was the same
hauling fertilizer to Memphis
stopping at the Toddle House
or the Villanova where a pork chop
cost more than a steak ought to
then off again
down the black top.

It was the same
on a Greyhound bus down '78
squeezing among the uniforms and hip flasks
walking the last ten miles
past the red schoolhouse and the soapstone gully
then off again
after the cotton was picked and to the gin.

Now it's all directions at once
with an air travel card
and a carry on bag
writing a speech working a budget
sweating a meeting chewing a tums
like a chicken with his head cut off
like a blind dog in a meat packing house.

Urban Flashback

Sitting somber in chauffeured cars,
surrounded by music and other people's stares,
wondering,
if I could go back
to laughing summer days
in '37 Chevrolet flat bed trucks
on dust-choking gravel roads.

Nodding with concern in padded conference rooms,
breathing cigar smoke and unscented deodorants,
wondering,
who here could recognize me
as I chopped at the threatening grass
and loosened the red sand soil
around the desperate cotton.

Smiling through dim rooms and light talk,
sipping something chic and soda,
wondering,
which of these ladies would bring
a covered dish and a quart of tea
to set among the prayers and songs
on the dinner grounds in the pine grove.

Dialogue with the Past

What are you doing here
in this conference room
out of the cotton fields and red dust
looking over the coffee and pads
lined yellow and legal size
pretending to be a company man?
What do you expect me to think
with your country church and preacher man rightness
nodding at the plan
smiling at the chart
acting like the profit margins make a damn
when I know where you come from?
Who do you think you're kidding
the cowshit just off your shoes
not far enough from overalls
to be happy in a collar
with *GQ* in the briefcase
a charge at Saks
and your grandfather restless in the cemetery
every time the closet opens?

Wait wait
I'm the same and it is too
and nothing changes but the words
when the CEO shuffles his feet
in their Italian leather loafers
and calls for further study
and appoints a task force
it's one of the county supervisors
in overalls and brogans
kicking the dust and saying
well fellers sometimes I think, well

then again I just don't know
And everybody goes off and thinks about it some more

But what are you trying to prove
when you didn't have a pot to pee in
or a window to throw it out of
when the roof leaked and the rats came in
and you looking now to shelter
your money as well as yourself?

Only that I still want what I wanted
when you cut through the shit
to do to get to hang on to something
and I only made the trade
country church for conference room
deacons for directors
and chicken in the pot for a few shares of stock

Smells of Life on Greyhound Buses during World War II

There was a salty ham one time
a prize from the country
during meat rationing.

It covered the sweat
and sour smells
of summer wet undershirts
of field worn overalls
of overdue diapers.

After a while it filled the bus with thoughts of food
and talk of hot biscuits
and butter and red eye gravy

> You-ever-have-them-big-dough-biscuit
> you-could-stick-a-finger-in
> and-poke-a-place-to-fill
> with-butter-and-jelly?

Suddenly
that ham made me center of the bus.
There was a staff sergeant
from Camp Currier, Missouri
and the old men called him sojer boy
and he became my friend
and patted the ham and said
he would cure his own again
when he got home from the war.

Sometimes now I wish for that salty smoky ham
but would it fit under the seats of 727s

on stratospheric routes
And could it work its aromatic magic
or would that man made unhuman air
blow it all away?

Shades of Gray

Seeing the old gray houses along every back road
lose the fight with vines and weeds
I think of when the old place burned
and shotgun shells went off
as we watched from the big rocks
the fire too hot to get closer
and wondered what Uncle Vee would say
about the place he was born
and his preacher daddy died

> *Never shoulda rented it*
> *now it's gone*

But I think it was better for the old place to burn
full of stuff and not deserted
empty in the woods
good for a picnic pilgrimage and not much else
gray and bent like a crazy old woman
widowed and grandwidowed and great grandwidowed
until no one knows who she is
or how much she meant in those days
how she grunted out children on corn shuck mattresses
and nursed them and wiped them
all the time cooking and washing and hoeing
and weeding and gathering and canning
and waiting for the next baby
all of them gone and their babies gone
her eyes gray and vacant
looking through a screen door
in the old folks' home
still wearing a bonnet to a ragged garden
chopping grass with a hoe so many years sharpened it's now a sliver

living for those times when someone young comes
and surrounds her with life for a while
then goes again
leaving her wondering if there'll be a next time
her life fading grayer and grayer
like a house with vines and brush
with rusty roof and sagging porch
with snakes and rats and coons and birds
but none of the life that gave it a reason to be.

So I'm glad the old place burned when it did
still filled with life
still sheltering love and the coming of children

Revival Meeting

How many heavy dusty nights
did I sit on wooden pews beside blonde sweating girls
stirring air toward them with funeral parlor fans
while infants slept finger sucking on quilts
and wasps flew heavy winged from lamp to lamp
searching for a place to fall and burn?

How many booming righteous promises of glory
did I ignore for whispered hints of ecstasy
while nervous deacons sun reddened in overalls
shouted self-conscious amens
and pale children pressed scared faces
into their mothers' laps?

How many stanzas of O Lamb of God I Come
did I sing on key and off
squirming with sweat sticking white shirt and khakis
still fanning and feeling that blonde warmth
while preachers pleaded voice catching phrases
and babies sucked late night breasts?

How many big and growing cousins
did I pat on work hardened backs
standing in the car fume night air
watching them twist hand rolled bull durhams into their lips
while bats swept wing dodging through the pole light
and blonde girls took sweat cooling walks?

How many veiled and wrinkled aunts
did I kiss on powdered cheeks
violet bath water smelling but sour
while blonde girls waited

on the pine needle ground beyond the tombstones
ready with slick and heavy tongue kisses?

And how many mornings have I sat
in the still warm and thick air of the empty church
reading the dim communion table carvings
while wasps not crisp dead like the others
flew in and out in and out
finding the lamps unlit and the sun too far away?

All Day Singing with Dinner on the Grounds

I

There were old men with ear trumpets
who patted their feet against the rhythm
and sang notes melodious only to themselves
sitting near the front on an aisle
where some young cousin or nephew had led them.
Snuff staining the corners of their mouths
tobacco breath filling the rows around them
they stayed there most of the day
but the rest of us moved in and out
and new groups came
in cars and trucks and yellow school buses

> *Here come*
> *Mr. Sanford Hale*
> *and the Philadelphia singers*

Coming to the singing convention
coming from three or four counties away
on dusty roads over hills and through bottoms
in heat that made the radiators boil
and fresh ironed shirts go damp and wrinkled
in heat that made the britches stick to our legs
when we got up from the hard oak pews.
Coming to sing
in duets and trios and quartets
and some soloists like Miss Ernestine Lee
whose face had the light of God in it
when she sang How Great Thou Art

> *I declare*
> *you can hear Jesus*
> *in her voice*

And some congregation singing
different song leaders from different churches
taking turns

> *Now we gonna ask*
> *Clyde Wyatt of Bethel Baptist*
> *to lead this next one*

And sometimes they'd get up a quartet
from different churches
always discussing who would sing lead and who would sing bass

> *Now you come on up here Leon*
> *and you too Hamer*
> *and you sing alto Mr. J. W.*

And after two or three false starts
they'd sing all the old ones
all the ones everybody knew and heard on the radio
every Sunday morning before church
On the Jericho Road and
Take a Little Walk with Jesus and
My God is Real and
I Saw the Light

Sometimes they'd make all the ladies sing a verse
or all the children
or all the folks over sixty
Then between songs there'd be testimonials
or one of the preachers would lead a prayer
because all the preachers from all the churches came
and led a prayer before the day was over.

Late in the morning
by some signal I never saw
the ladies began to leave the church and go to the cars
and get baskets and snacks
and head to the dinner grounds,
big gray tables under the trees
or sometimes rough lumber nailed between the trees,
and spread starched table cloths
and decide somehow among themselves
where the meat would be
and the vegetables and bread
where to gather the cakes and pies
and jugs of iced tea.
Then someone would let the song leader know
and he'd say that dinner was ready
and everybody would go outside and have another song and a prayer
then start along the tables
smiling at their neighbors
thanking God for the day
spooning their plates full

    Now you boys just keep back
    and let them ladies go first

It seemed all the food in the world
fried chicken crisp and soggy
country ham and sausage in biscuits
deviled eggs and creamed corn
and black-eyed peas and okra
and green beans and sliced tomatoes
and cornbread and spoon bread
and all manner of pies and cakes
stacked apple pies and Mississippi mud pies

pound cakes sliced thick with strawberries and cream
big wet banana cakes
and coconut cakes you ate with a spoon.
And the ladies would watch to see
whose dishes got eaten first

> *Miss Nora*
> *you just can't make enough*
> *of them old time buttermilk pies*

and smile and say how this wasn't near as good
as they usually make.

III

Then the singing would start again
with people coming and going
with men and boys standing outside the open windows
rolling cigarettes from little sacks of tobacco
picking their teeth with black gum brushes
and spitting into the red powder dust.
And later in the afternoon
we'd go off into the pines behind the church
and throw rocks
and shoot green plums from our slingshots
and not really listen to the singing any more
but hear it anyway
and the motors starting
and the people getting on the school buses
and our names called when it was time to go.

Baptism

He waded into the cold water up to his knees
then across a sandbar and into the current
and turned and called to us
and suddenly the swimming hole was different.
We'd been there for a thousand swims
but it was different
colder maybe
swifter
deeper
surrounded not by boys and girls in swimsuits
but by Sunday dressed ladies and coat and tied men
singing

> *Shall we gather at the river*
> *the beautiful the beautiful*
> *river*

And we moved in a line
barefoot and in white shirts and wash pants
the girls in dark colored dresses
which would not show through when they got wet
Across the shallows onto the sandbar
and from there went one at a time
in the name of the father, the son, and the holy ghost
to be put under the water
his arm behind our shoulders
and his hand over our mouth and nose
and our hand on his hand
For only a few seconds but it seemed longer
longer than any time when we had jumped or dropped from a vine
longer than when we swam underwater to scare the girls
longer than we thought we could ever stand

but he pulled us up
and said amen and the people said hallelujah
and our mothers hugged us as we went wet onto the bank.

Then he came out of the water
and we sang On Jordan's Stormy Banks I Stand
and he lifted his arms over us
all shivering there
the water draining from our pants cuffs
dresses clinging to the girls' legs

And said some words
about our sins washed away
and cleansed in the blood
and born again
And told us we were saved
and would go to heaven
and have life everlasting
and many other important things
we remembered for a long time.

Death in the Family

I

People hug us and cry
and pray we'll be strong
and know we'll see her again someday
And we nod and they pat and rub
reassuring her to heaven

> *She's with Jesus now*
> *no suffering where she is*

Then sit on hard benches and sing of precious memories how they linger
and farther along we'll understand it

> *Cheer up my brother*
> *We're not forgotten*

The preacher studies his Bible and stares at the ceiling
and the song leader in his blue funeral suit sweats
and strokes the air
with a callused hand

> *We'll understand it*
> *all by and by*

And powdered and rosy cheeked
Miss Anne sleeps in an open coffin
the children standing tiptoe to see through the flowers
but scared to go near and drawing back when lifted
And the choir brings a balm in Gilead
and a roll is called up yonder

When the trumpet of the lord shall sound
and time shall be no more

And big men shake heads white at the hat line
while women weep and flutter air with palm leaf fans
And later we stand amidst the stones
by the mound of red clay
our eyes wet against the sun
and listen to preachers and mockingbirds
and the 23rd Psalm

II

Men stand uneasy in ties
and nod their hats to ladies
and kick gravel with shoes too tight
and talk about life

> *Nobody no better'n Miss Anne*
> *No Sir*
> *No Sir*

Smoking bull durhams around the porch
shaking their heads to agree
and sucking wind through their teeth

> *Never let you go thirsty*
> *bring a jugga tea to the field*
> *every day*

They open doors for us and look at the ground
as if by not seeing our faces they become invisible
There are not enough chores
so three draw well water
and two get the mail

and four feed the dogs
and the rest chop wood
and wish for something to say

> *Lester broke his arm one time*
> *and Miss Anne plowed that mule*
> *like a man*
> *put in the whole crop*

And they talk of crops and plowing
of rain and sun and flood and drought
The seasons passing in memory
marking changes in years and lives
that men remember at times
when there's nothing to say

III

Ladies come with sad faces
and baskets of sweets
teacakes, pecan pies, puddings, memories
and we choose and they serve
telling stories and god blessing the children

> *I declare that Miss Anne*
> *was the sweetest Christian person*
> *in the world*

Saying all the things to be said
doing all the things to be done
like orderly spirits
freshening beds from the grieving night
poking up fires gone cold
filling the table and sideboard

then gathering there to urge and cajole
as if the dead rest easier on our full stomachs

Lord how Miss Anne would have loved that country ham

No sadness so great it cannot be fed away
by the insistent spirits

That banana cake is her very own recipe
I remember how she loved my spoon bread
She canned the berries in this cobbler

And suddenly we are transformed
and eat and smile and thank you
and the ladies nod and know they have done well again
in time of need
And the little girls watch and learn
And we forget the early spring cemetery
and the church with precious memories
and farther along we do understand it
the payments and repayments
of all the ladies that were and are
and we pray ever will be. Amen

Prayer for a Country Preacher

Oh God
let him go dreaming when he goes
let him go preaching a revival meeting
with the congregation eager beyond discomfort
on a wet and insect laden night

let him go singing bass
on a Sunday morning
his head above the others
his voice bringing power beyond
power in the blood

let him go walking the river bottom
leading the lost fishermen through the storm
breaking saplings to mark the trail

let him go wading the shallows
his boots sucking mud in the dawn
calling the green headed mallard
shooting quick and sure

Not bad for a country preacher

let him go praying
at a table of summer Sunday food
fried chicken and sliced tomatoes
and peas and cornbread and tea
with his family around him
like disciples

Oh God if he must go
let him go dreaming

Death Message

How long have I waited
for this late night phone ringing?
To come awake knowing
and to lie awake thinking
And it came on a night
when I heard a far-off train
calling in two tones
letting everyone know it was
moving on down the line.

Far off trains and dying people
roll together through my life
as if no one in Mississippi
can die without a mourning train
to start the dogs howling
to set loose all the sounds
of a world turned sad.

In that night and dawning
unreal rafters reveal themselves
above the bed
a thin memory of rough sawn boards
and dawns under a tin roof.
Then a jet whines
no mourning train but a space machine
returning me to a lifetime ago.

Against All Those Desperate Prayers

Against all those desperate prayers
whispered in airplanes
and hospital corridors
Against all those deals and bargains
of new beginnings and new behaviors I thought God
could not afford to pass up
Against all the wild promises
he died anyway.

From
Life after Mississippi
(1989)

Fishing Day

I

Old ladies in bonnets fished
with cane poles,
baiting their hooks with worms
or grubs from under a wet log
turned over by one of us boys.
They sat,
long sleeved against the mosquitos
and watched cork bobbers
and caught small bream,

> *Lord, they are the sweetest little fish.*
> *Fry 'em crispy and eat 'em*
> *bones and all*

tossing them in a bucket
where they splashed and swam a while
then turned belly up,
their gills moving in and out
slowly until they died.

II

We would go to the bottom early,
in a mule wagon,
men and boys and women and girls
and babies and dogs and all,
and the men and boys would find
a flat dry place
and start fires and cut green brush,

and the women and girls would spread quilts
and sometimes make a mosquito net tent
for the babies
but most times would just fan them,
or we'd build shelters of branches
if it looked like a sprinkle,
and always a big cooking fire.
We brought flour sacks and tow sacks
full of iron skillets
and salt and cornmeal and lard.
We brought plates and knives and forks and glasses.
There were gallon jugs of tea
and always cakes and pies.

III

But we couldn't eat until we caught fish,
not little bream but catfish,
blues and willows and yellows and channels,
on set hooks.
First some of us cut saplings or cane
then trimmed and sharpened the ends
while others seined for bait
in the little sloughs and backwaters
left from when the river flooded.

> *You boys watch for cottonmouths,*
> *they like them sloughs.*

Then we'd unroll our hooks
one at a time,

big claw hooks on heavy cotton cord
with nuts and washers and whatever else
for weight,
and tie them to the poles.
Under a low-hanging tree was good
or the downstream side of a log
or around a drift,

> *Mind you don't set so close in there,*
> *he'll hang you on a branch and slip away*

jamming the sharpened end of the pole
deep into the mud bank,

> *Stick it deep, boys.*
> *I lost a pole one time that was a foot*
> *in the bank. Pulled it out and swam off.*

then pushing the pole down parallel to the water
until the hook touched bottom
and the line bowed,
then up just a few inches.

> *Come and get it, Mr. Catfish.*

IV

When we had set maybe a hundred hooks
we seined more bait,
then we ran the hooks,
moving along the slick bank,
checking each hook, rebaiting,
always hoping the next pole
would be jerking,
slapping the water,

then arguing over whose turn it was
to land the fish.

V

The women who did not fish sat on quilts
and fanned with palm leaf
or funeral parlor fans
and talked about the heat
or the mosquitos or something they heard at church.
And they yelled at the children
to stay back from the bank.

> *You slide in that water*
> *we'll never see you again.*

And sometimes one might sing a church song
while the others listened or hummed,
and one might do some sewing,

> *I swear, Nora, you make*
> *the straightest little stitches.*

and they would watch
how the fishing was going
and tend the cooking fire
until the coals were right.

VI

The men never wanted to eat
because they came to fish
but the little children would get fussy
and the women would spread a place,

Boys, better clean some of them fish

and we would punch a hole
at the back of the catfish's head
and run a broom straw down his backbone.

Paralyzes 'em.

then cut the skin enough to grab it with pliers
and pull it right down to his tail,
first breaking his fins at the base.

Git them fins before they git you.

With a big one,
at least ten pounds,
we'd nail him to a tree,
through the head,
then make the cut and skin him.
The guts were a mess
but we kept some parts for bait,
the only fun of it
seeing what was in his stomach.
You'd be surprised what we found sometimes,
a whole turtle, shell and all,
a little snake,
one time a mouse,
and the girls hated it.

VII

The women would roll catfish steaks
in cornmeal
then put them in a skillet of hot lard,

with sliced potatoes in another,
and hushpuppies after the fish,
and the girls would get out the slaw and tea.

Boys run git the men
and tell 'em we're ready
for the blessing.

And we would bow our heads
while a deacon gave thanks
for the day and the fish
and the fellowship,
and blessed the food to the good
of our bodies, amen.

VIII

In the afternoon there were naps
and more fishing
and quiet talking
and sometimes a rain shower
which nobody minded
and which usually made the fish bite better.

Look at 'em. They're loading on.

all of us wondering why that was.
Then we'd begin to load the wagon,
the men arguing about
whether to take up the lines
or bait them overnight
and come back in the morning.
We always left the hooks
because no one could resist the possibility

On Paying Attention

of coming tomorrow and finding
a pole bent into the water
straining against the biggest catfish
we would ever see.

Mister Mac

People didn't know how to take Mister Mac,
"whip-poor-will" they called him
because his nose made him look like one,
and laughed when he ran,
the only Republican in the county.

Feel we need a two-party system.

Still, something was sad about his twenty or so votes,
though he said it was more
than he had family,

Musta convinced a few.

and went on about his business,
writing insurance
for companies who wished
they could get someone else,
but nobody in the territory
wanted to bump Mister Mac
out of the job,
his being the only support for his sisters,
and most of the people having gone to school to him
at one time or another,
back when he was one of the few educated men
in the area,
though even then they didn't know whether to admire
or feel sorry for him
because it was not easy to be educated
and amount to much in those days.
So they called him whip-poor-will
and dodged his car

when he drove, cataracts and all,
to the square,
where he would soften them up
with humor,

> *You never been choked*
> *till you been choked on a sweet tater.*

then tell all who would listen
how the South would never rise again
without a two-party system,
ending with his favorite story.

> *One time the judge asked this man,*
> *"Henry, what you got to say*
> *before I sentence you to hang*
> *by the neck till dead?"*
> *Henry said, "Judge, I just*
> *want to say it sure is gonna*
> *be a lesson to me."*

But "peculiar" was the word they used,
not eccentric, like nowadays;
"kinda peculiar," they'd say.
Mister Mac thought they admired his spunk
despite how they treated him,

> *Trying their best not to listen,*
> *they hear me though.*

but when he died and his cousin sobbed
all through the service
and told me, "Jimmy there's not a dry eye
in this town today,"
the preacher had to ask the people

to bunch up in the front
so it would look like a crowd.

Cousin El

When I remember my childhood Mississippi
I think of Cousin El
who lost his sight to a sweet gum ball
and lived the rest of his life on the home place.
Did he always see those hills and fields and trees
as they were when he was a child
throwing sweet gum balls with his brothers?
And will I always see that place
as it was,
sweet and green and dusty,
and not as it is now,
a kind of blindness protecting me
from the video stores and pizza shops
and straightened rivers
and thinned forests?

The answers are yes and yes,
but here's the difference:
I indulge the blindness,
and Cousin El would have loved to see the changes,
ugliness and all.

Grabblin'

I

The word is grappling
but we said grabblin'
and bragged that Mississippi
was the only state with a season for it,
our real boast being that Mississippi
was the only state
with men and boys brave enough to do it,
to crouch in the water
and reach up under the bank,
bare-handed,
searching a slick hole
hoping for a catfish
and not a snake or snapper or dogfish
or any of the dangers
we knew could be under those waters.

II

We went in big groups,

> *Don't ever grabble by yourself, boys,*
> *a 15-pound catfish can drown you.*
> *He's got you much as you got him.*

six or eight men and that many boys,
in overalls and barefoot
or wearing our most wore-out shoes,
starting miles up the river
and wading the shallows,
which was most of it,
dropping into holes here and there,

waist or shoulder deep,
to poke around sunken logs or drifts
or under the mud banks.

III

Every boy had to catch a catfish,
sticking a thumb in the sandpaper mouth
and fingers in the gills,
pulling him from his den
where the precious eggs lay.

> *Be sure you got those gills*
> *or he'll spin on your thumb*
> *and peel the skin like a onion.*

We'd put our catch in big tow sacks
dragging them behind us in the water
and when we rested we'd open the sacks
and tell our stories

> *That there jughead*
> *got a piece of my thumb.*

remembering each fish and its part of the river.
Grabblin' was for big fish
and we caught twenty- and thirty-pounders,
sometimes two men wrestling one
onto the bank
then resting out of breath
at the work of it.

IV

There may have been a thousand snakebites
and there may have been none;
though we boys expected snakes in every hole
our fear of shame was stronger than our fear of snakes.

> *Stick your hand on in there, boys,*
> *a snake'll run from you,*
> *you couldn't touch one if you tried.*

We saw so many on the bank
and dropping from tree limbs as we moved toward them
that we held our breath
every time we reached into a hole
or we pretended to talk to the fish
the way the men did

> *Okay, Mr. Catfish, I need me something*
> *to make the gravy stink tonight.*

V

Sometimes a grabblin' would end
with a fish fry or big stew,
the women and girls gathering with all the food,
except fish,
in Ira's pasture where we would wade
out of the river
and dump our sacks onto the grass.
Then we'd clean fish
and change clothes
and show our blooded thumbs
to the little boys
and the girls,

telling them yes we saw snakes
but you can't worry about stuff like that
if you want to be a grabbler.

When Boys Wanted to Go to War

When I sneaked the flashlight under the covers
and read comics
until the precious batteries were weak,
I learned all how to hate my enemies.

First
on those pages
with the shadow pictures of babies on bayonets
with their mothers looking terrified
while demonic Nazis and Japs
prepared to stick their gleaming daggers
you know where,
with the Nazi pilots
shouting, "Die you swine,"
as they machine-gunned our pilots
parachuting from their burning
Lightnings or Mustangs or Spitfires.

Then
in church where
someone's son or brother was dead
and there was no turning the other cheek.

And
in a dozen hot red dust cemeteries
with honor guards and seven-gun salutes
making the babies wake and cry,
where there were little brothers itching
to grab those honor guard rifles
and load them with real bullets
and go get those dirty murderers.

And some little brothers did go
and some were too young
but went to Boy Scouts
and did close order drill like the army,
and hoped the war would last a long time.

Leaving Mississippi

Part of me never left
and another part is always leaving,
leaving Mississippi but never gone.
"Jimmy when you gonna come on back
down home," my people ask,
and I cannot say, "Never,
I've found my home somewhere else"
any more than I can say my home
was never in the State of Mississippi
but in the community of it,
in my father's churches,
in Abel's store,
in Ashland on the square,
in how the people were together.
Now my home is gone forever from Mississippi—
yet it is with me still,
in the fall smell of wood smoke
from some suburban chimney,
in an Atlanta taxi driver's turn of phrase,
in the quiet of an old church in Bavaria,
in the call of an Iowa night hawk,
in a fish breaking the surface of a Colorado stream,
in the night peepers everywhere
in a stanza of Amazing Grace,
in the crickets,
in dust.

Saying Goodbye

Every time I say goodbye to the old folks
I know it may be the last time,
and when it turns out to be,
I am still surprised
and regret the things I did not say,
so now I machine-gun the news to them,
everything I said at the past goodbye
and will say at the next one,
as if loading them with stories
and recollections
to take along
if they go before I return.

Yet I know I still will regret
the things I did not say,
the words that would cloud us up
and make us look at our shoes
and cause one of them to say,
"Aw save that talk till they're ready
to put me in the ground."

So I keep those words to myself,
not wanting anyone to think
I see death coming.

"Your Uncle Vee Had a Massive Stroke Last Night"

June 23, 1987

Poem 1.

I always throw the number away
as if I'll never need it again,
then comes a call
and I dial the old 601-555-1212
and ask for Tippah County Hospital,
hearing those seven digits I've heard so often,
then punching the buttons,
dreading the voices,
dreading the things that won't be said.

Poem 2.

Uncle Vee is the last one now,
and I wonder if he's the only man in Mississippi
who still lives in a house he built
of raw lumber sixty years ago,
who plowed a mule in red clay,
over and around hills,
not a flat spot on the place,
who cursed crows in the garden
and hawks and foxes and chicken snakes,
who killed hogs and cured meat and smoked it,
who ate pork and greens and cornbread,
and drank gallons of buttermilk,
and got bigger and bigger
but at eighty-six was still hungry every day,
who taught six grades in the same red schoolhouse

On Paying Attention

before it was blown to bits by the Second Army
on maneuvers in Holly Springs National Forest,
who taught singing school
and led the choir
and took busloads of singers
to singing conventions all around five counties,
who served in the legislature
where he wore a tie every day,
and who was cheated out of the election
by a kind of politics he thought was a sin.

Poem 3.

Now Uncle Vee wants to go home,
he wants to sing hymns,
he wants to feel a plow breaking the ground,
he wants to drive his old car to the store
and talk about the weather
and buy somebody a belly washer
and smell the hoop cheese and coal oil.
He wants to see his wife
ironing in her straight wash dress,
wiping sweat with the back of her hand.
He wants to smell her biscuits
and put a dipper in the sweet water
she brings from the cistern.
He wants to hear his children
playing around the porch.
So he tries,
he wakes and pulls at the tubes
when the nurses aren't looking,
and cries when finally I reach him
on the telephone.

Mortality

It's my turn to become my father,
liver spots, knotty hands and all,
time for me to tell my stories so many times
that someone thinks he should tape-record them
for his grandchildren
who will never know me.
Verdell is already his father
and I have heard his stories
of Calhoun and Leroy and Jimmie Lee
and I have turned on the tape recorder,
a sure sign.

Flavors

It happened again
this time with blackberry jelly and bacon,
together like a cold morning
on the farm
the fire popping and someone stamping his feet,
and troves of warmth here and there,
in front of the fireplace, around the kitchen stove,
from a bed with the covers thrown back.

It happened this time in one of those places
with toasted white bread
and grilled bacon cured with a needle
instead of in a smokehouse,
and Knott's Berry Farm blackberry preserves
from a one-serving jar,
even an orchid on the table.

Yet I could squint at those far from home palm trees,
and despite the china and crystal,
my pressed cuffs, dry-blown hair and Old-Spice smell,
could squeeze the blackberry and bacon
between my tongue and the roof of my mouth,
tasting and tasting,
all the old flavors again.

Ordination

for the Rev. Ms. Patricia Ryan

Brother Jim Thompson came,
the oldest,
with overalls and a white shirt buttoned at the collar,
with a walking cane and a Bible
that had stood fifty years of pounding,
and with that old fire burning through his cataracts.

> *Didn't need no seminary.*
> *Always preached the Bible*
> *and the Lord Jesus Christ*
> *crucified and buried and*
> *raised from the dead.*

Brother Hamer came
and Brother Ewart
and the three Walker boys,
preachers all.
They came through rain,
wrestling the wheels of their out-of-county cars,
sliding in ruts so deep the tail pipes dragged.
They parked under the trees
and along the road,
then walked, shined shoes and all,
through the mud,
picking their way along the high spots
like children jumping puddles.
Into the church of their fathers,
the place they had all felt the call,
the old home church
where thousands of hands had pressed
on the bowed heads of new preacher boys,

On Paying Attention

of sun-reddened young men called by the Lord,
called from the cotton fields to preach the word.
They had felt the hands,
these old preachers,
felt those blunt-fingered, work-hardened hands,
felt them like a blessing,
like an offering,
like a burden.
Felt them at weddings and baptizings,
felt them in the heat of a summer revival sermon,
in the agony of a baby's funeral,
in the desperate prayer against some killer disease,
in the frustrating visit with a mind gone senile.

And now the old preachers had come to lay their hands
on the head of a new kind of preacher,
a preacher from the seminary,
a preacher who studied the Bible in Greek and Hebrew,
who knew about religions they never heard of,
who knew about computers
and memory banks full of sermons
and many other modern things.
A new kind of preacher,
and yet,
a preacher who still would feel on her head
the hands
like a commandment
from all the preachers and deacons who ever were.

Goodbye Truck Stop Girls

I

There was one not far from New Albany
named Velma
who could do the dirty boogie on one foot
all the way to the floor and up again
if you would feed the jukebox
and her pocket.

And there were others
named Mavis and Erlene and Wilma
and Inez and Bettyanne
and Lottie Sue and Sara Vee
and they could all boogie and jitterbug
and wait tables at the same time
and take care of themselves
no matter what anybody said.

And the ones who didn't marry some old boy
and have babies
to bring back and show off
to the cooks and cashiers and other girls
got older and meaner
and started using coarse words
when we would feed the juke
and warned the younger girls about us
and then went on to do whatever they do
always in another town.

II

But something happened:
the juke music changed

and good old boys became cowboys
and the truck stop girls put on tight jeans
and cowboy boots
and talked about snorting toot
and asked the truck cowboys for bennies
and yellowjackets and stuff we never heard of
and broke out in a bunch of names
like Debbie and Lynn and Tammie
and Dawn and Renaé
and Tanya and Crystal
and squealed into CB radios
for cowboys to stop in
and would hardly wait on anybody
and would never dance to the juke
no matter how many quarters were pumped.

Television and the Church

Every time I find myself in the little church
where my grandfather and father
preached,
where my uncle led singing conventions
while someone played an upright piano
and pumped an old organ;
every time I feel the air-conditioning
and hear the latest hit
from the Top Forty Christian Countdown,
I think,
Damn you, television.

Mississippi Writers Day

The irony was lost on no one.
There we sat,
poets, writers, teachers, scholars,
in the chamber where some
of our grandfathers and great-grandfathers
deliberated on how to solve
the nigra problem,
then passed the poll tax
and set up separate but equal schools
and decided that everyone had to read
and understand the Constitution
before he could vote.
We sat there,
in the chamber in the building
whose bricks were made by slaves.
We sat and listened
to black poets,
to angry black poets
who read their words
so that no one could ever feel safe
reading them in a white voice.

It was a lesson about words
and how their color changes.
It was a lesson about places
and how their power changes.
It was a lesson about people
and how their fear changes.

Elegy for a Gentle Person

She was sitting on the porch
in a cane bottom chair
leaning against the wall by the front door
watching them shoot blanks at the red schoolhouse
and throw smoke bombs through its windows,
her daddy shaking his head and cursing,

> *Reckon we'll win this war*
> *if the Japs hole up in a schoolhouse*

when the soldier came around the cistern
and stole her heart
just like in the stories.
Later, some said he was ignorant and worthless,
a lazy no count,
and she was the only one surprised
when he left after the children were born.
But back then he was handsome
in the uniform
and even her daddy saw new possibilities.

Everyone said God knows she tried
but what could you expect
from a man with no class at all,
and some worried about how the children
would turn out
but she was from a good family
and was a hard-working mother.
Money was scarce and after a while
so were her healthy days,
heart trouble, they said,
and long times not able to work.

But she did not complain
even when the children grew up and moved out,
and if she ever thought about her soldier
she did not say.

Some said her life was small
and she must have been lonely
and how could she have kept going,
but she did not ask these questions,
busy as she was
going to church when she felt up to it,
watching the TV,
helping her mother and daddy in their age,
sitting sometimes on that same porch
across the road from where
the schoolhouse had been—
now a flat spot so barren
that no one could ever imagine
there had been children
and games
and laughter
and bells.

Funeral for a Gentle Person

Behind the coffin,
flowing from the pews,
brother, sister, children, grandchildren, cousins, aunts,
a river of kinship bears her
to a place we hope she dreamed about,
all those days alone
in a small house
by the side of a busy road,
no cars stopping.

Life after Mississippi

I

The question always hanging
behind my head is
"Can I make it to Mississippi?"
Every old car I've looked at and bought,
"Will this baby make it to Mississippi?"
Every tank of gas
will almost get me back to Mississippi.
Every paycheck has to be enough
at least for a bus ticket
even though I don't want to go.
Long ago I could have stopped worrying,
but now it could be war
or the great depression
or cancer
sending me back into the family land,
where I'd walk through a woodsy bottom,
a world as far away as it used to be,
and I would garden and hunt
and fish clean streams,
and eat catfish and bream with no spots in their flesh,
and store onions and potatoes in a root cellar,
and be a neighbor to everyone
for as long as we lasted.

II

I know a crease between the hills
where water comes from under a rock.
A little digging
and I'd have a spring
where I would take my bucket to fill every day
and leave a gourd so others could drink.

III

Sooner or later
the snake would come
but this time things would be different.
I would let him coil
in the top of that fallen pine,
his hourglass markings dark as death,
and against everything I've ever been taught,
would step around him,
no rock, no stick, no gun,
just staying alive in Mississippi.

New Birth

for Sally, Spring 1984

From her sure knowledge
that everything would come out all right,
things began to come out all right,
out through the present day horrors,
through my fears and loss and grief,
through the demons lurking around everything I do.

As if directly from that optimism,
Ronald came unconcerned into the cold and light,
no longer surrounded by the sounds of Sally's life,
but sliding easily into the doctor's bloody hands
then snuggling back onto his mother's warmth,
none of his father's wailing against the world,
none of that waiting for the next shoe to fall.

And I count toes and fingers
and check his little penis
and touch the soft spot on his head
and watch the doctor probe and squeeze,
not believing everything came out all right.

Later I wonder how these years have come
from pain to death to pain to life
to what next?
A baby babbling in the backpack,
a mother walking her healthy pace,
a dog trailing behind
and me holding on,
through the neighborhood, through everything,
with each day
one by one
coming out all right.

On Paying Attention

There came a time in my volunteer life
when I began to give in
to the seductions of righteousness
and to think of my work as a sacrifice
for the good of others.
I would make schedules no one should try
so that people would ask
how it was possible for one man to do so much.
It was a time of three speeches
and three cities
in one day,
and in all the scurrying
I did not want the delay
of a restroom conversation
with a hesitant little man
in a cheap new suit.
I needed a quick pee, five minutes to think,
and two minutes to get to the podium.
But there he was,
with the side effects I knew so well,
the puffy cheeks, the swollen gums
as he smiled and told me he had a job now
and hadn't had a seizure in six months.
I gave him the quick back pat
and the smile,
never expecting to see him again.
But he sat in the front row
and smiled a greeting when I rose to speak,
the dignitary from the national office,
bringing word from Washington,
the National Commission,
the Hill, the White House.

He smiled too often
and over-nodded and made too much of his notes,
clicking his pen and turning pages,
back and forth,
as if studying what he'd written.
When our eyes met he smiled and nodded,
another guy, I thought, who wants people
to think he knows the speaker.
So I avoided looking at him
until he shuffled, crossed his legs,
and stretched them in front of him.
When I saw the soles of his shoes,
slightly soiled, less than a day worn,
I realized he had bought the suit and shoes
just for this meeting,
just to hear a speech squeezed
into an afternoon between two other cities.
He had looked forward to it,
planned for it,
put new job money into it,
and would make notes
so that he could remember always
what the important man came to teach.

But the lesson was mine to learn—
about sacrifice
and counting blessings,
about patience
and paying attention to teachers
wherever I find them.

Airport Scene I.

She had country girl written all over her,
except on her T-shirt
which said "I'm terrific,"
but I know she never said terrific
until she came to the city
and went to secretary school
and learned to dress and make up
then got a job
and tried to be terrific
enough to marry a new salesman
now getting off a plane
on Friday night,
too tired for the baby on her hip
and wondering if his wife's body
will ever be terrific again.

Airport Scene II.

It used to be train stations
but now it's airports,
the core sample of humanity,
rushing always and waiting,
crying hellos and goodbyes.
Think about that,
how high and fast they go,
machines full of people,
miracle rays guiding them everywhere on earth,
billions of dollars of invisible signals
bringing the people down safely
so they can rush and wait
and cry their hellos and goodbyes,
just like in the train stations.

Airport Scene III.

I know a traveler in a hurry,
always fidgeting in the rampway,
who wants to paint a red line
on the floor at every gate
and announce "No hugging or kissing
before you reach the red line"
so other people,
especially him,
won't be delayed by all that affection.

Airport Scene IV.

Infants they say have a special filter
that shuts down the hearing
when the world gets too loud,
letting them sleep through
jack hammers or rock and roll,
an enviable gift, I think,
rushing through an airport,
but reserved for infants
because they would not be able
to deal with the noise,
and would scream
at the engines
and metal announcements
and whistles and horns.

But when the body grows
we hear it all
whether we can deal with it or not,
a random thought,
seeing a retarded woman in the crosswalk,
amidst the horns and whistles and yells,
her father at her side,
her eyes moving without focus,
her body jerking against the noise,
like a shot rabbit against the pellets,
but the father squeezing and patting,
his head close,
pouring his "okay" and "good" and "almost there"
into her ear,
love filtering the noise.

Widow

She told the children
they didn't have to keep going to the same church,
they could take their children to a bigger church,
with a gym and a pool,
not reminding them their father was still
fertilizing the azaleas
where he had been scattered,
white dust on a rainy day,
drifting under the black umbrellas
after we dug our hands into the urn
and broadcast him
like seed
among the flowers
then walked to the cars
and noticed him
like talcum
on our shoes and around our cuffs,
and later found he had come home with us,
under our fingernails,
then before supper
scrubbed with those little stiff bristle brushes
and tried to wash him away.

Listening to Old Wounds

A man I love is going crazy
they say,
but he says it's only his hearing.

> *Get a hearing aid,* I say
and he says,
> *Then people shout at you.*
And I say,
> *I am shouting.*

He knows the truth
but tells me he used to have good ears,

> *I could hear a whine on the line*
> *a hundred yards away.*
> *Knew just which pole to climb.*

and that the Japs ruined his hearing
in New Guinea,
the night they parachuted
right on top of his unit,
silent among the foxholes,
all of them lost in the dark,
shouting passwords and trusting no one.

> *I had to listen too hard*
> *that night. A twig cracking.*
> *Anything.*

After the fighting he sat
for weeks
pounding an Australian coin with

a soup spoon
until the coin became a ring
which he sent me,
too big then
but which I wore for years.
Now he doesn't remember the ring,
and when I mention it
he cocks his head and squints,
as if listening for the memory,
but he hears only
"them damn jabbering yellow monkeys"
drifting above him,

> *They didn't know*
> *we were down there and we couldn't tell*
> *where the voices were coming from.*

then dropping among his buddies,
the shooting and screaming,
the silence,
life depending on his ears.

I can understand why they say
he's going crazy.
It has something to do with all the sounds,
heartbeats, footsteps, breathing,
out there somewhere,
who knows how far away,
but still listened for—
still listened for.

MADRAP**

for Jimmy

This is a place of daily miracles
where strangers sit in circles
and discover the lost language of love,
putting themselves back together,
fitting tears and anger and pain
like puzzle pieces
until their stories make sense again.

**Mercy Alcohol and Drug Rehabilitation Program, M.A.D.R.P., pronounced "Madrap"
by those in the program.

Hospital Visits

Under my arm is a blue folder
stuffed with everything I could ever learn
about booze and dope
except how to feel when
sitting in a circle with other children
it comes his turn and he says
"I'm Jim, an alcoholic and drug addict."

Next to me in the elevator is a couple with a pillow
for sitting on the floor
in a circle with other couples
learning to strain and grunt and breathe
another child into birth.

In the slow and acrid elevator
I want to tell them everything
about how it never ends,
being a parent,
about how it transforms you forever,
beyond celebration or pain or death.

But this is not the time or place
for a born again father to make his speech,
so I say "good luck"
and pray safe deliverance for us all.

Baptism

There's something about this,
about putting the people under the water
and raising them up
in the name of the Father, the Son, and the Holy Ghost,
something that makes the people cry,
that makes them want to want
everything to be all right,
that makes them want to leave this place
and be better,
to immerse themselves in their lives
and somehow be washed clean
of all the things they think
they should not have done
and should not still want to do.
That's it.
Not the other stuff,
the star in the east,
the treasures in heaven,
or any of the old stories.
Not even life after death.
It is only to be new again.

Present Day Horrors

The present day horrors
would be bad enough in themselves,
abstractly,
but it's the little scenes of desperation and despair
playing through everything
that finally get us:
A Kleenex full of phlegm

> *Save that. Don't throw it away.*
> *(I won't.)*
> *They don't believe I cough up stuff.*
> *Save it. Show them.*
> *(I will.)*

And the nurse comes and I give it to her
with all the urgency I can feign

> *See*
> *They said there was nothing there.*

And he grins and nods
knowing they will believe him now.

Later I see a tiny light of recognition
after the lung collapses and I come
in the midst of the struggle
wondering how and when it will end
watching that wild stare over the respirator mask
seeing all the energy go with every breath,
none to spare for the hello nod,
only enough for one more breath,
and one more.

Then someone says

When the eyes get dry it's over.

and I wonder what that means
watching the eyes dryer and dryer
until something very small changes
and I think

Shit he's not here now.
He's not staying for this part.

the spaces between breaths growing
until that's all there is.

And that last space fills with memories
of little struggles in the middle of the night,
of incoherent sentences
like "oh why now pee"
and I hold his penis and point it into the bedpan
as he used to hold mine those years ago
when he was the adult and I was the child.
And he is embarrassed
and I am embarrassed for him
but we smile,
a last signal that after all this
we're still together
through these little scenes,
through the phlegm
and urine and blood and oxygen
and hypos and IVs,
through every pun and every game
and every old joke,
right up to the lung-crushing eye-drying end.

The Wig

It was if he had not even tried
for a match,
the way the ads promise,
using real human hair
to match what was there before,
and we didn't know what to say
when he limped into the office,
then he laughed,
"Hell, with the doctor bills,
who can afford a decent rug?"
and we realized it was his last big joke.
One day the wig was short, another long,
then he changed colors,
then blacked a tooth,
"always clowning," we would say later,
shaking our heads and smiling,
"right up to the end."
But as usual we missed the point,
about how people pay more attention to a clown
than to a dying man.

Camping Memories

Surrounded by a deep and warm night
we breathed into each other's hair.
Life moved around us and between us,
creatures and feelings waked and stirred
making quiet and simple sounds.
There were no predators.
Reptiles did not bite
and insects did not sting.

In John Maguire's Garden
Claremont, May 15, 1988

Very formal in places
because some people need the predictability,
this garden still has wild spots which draw me,
like a raucous chorus of Amazing Grace
late after some distinguished dinner,
or an eyebrow twisting upward
below a mortar board,
unexpected, distracting, beyond cultivation.

Some might hurry to prune the overgrown places,
to soften the surprise
of coming upon life so extravagant
that it outblooms the boundaries.
But not me, John,
not me.
I believe the gardener knew what he was doing.

On Paying Attention

Reminiscence at Toul
July 18, 1987

Thirty years ago
on New Year's eve
drunk on French champagne
we shot bottle rockets
from the windows
of Hank and Willi's
rented chateau overlooking Nancy.

It sounds so worldly
which is how we wanted to think of ourselves,
but Lord, we were just children,
sent by the government to fly airplanes
and to save western Europe
from World War III.

We thought we had all the important things
still left to do
and were just playing at importance
for the time being.
It never occurred to us,
living in our community of friends,
having first babies,
seeing husbands die,
helping young widows pack to go home,
that we had already started the important things.
What could we have been thinking,
or perhaps it's how could we have known
that times get no better,
that important things come without background music,
that life is largely a matter of paying attention?

Tannois

for Adam Growald, July 21, 1987, aboard The Princess

At the lavois
down the hill from her house
she tells about the day
she saved the
Americans from the rain,
two men, two women, and a child,
un petit garcon,
nineteen months old the mother said,
on bicycles in the rain,
and she tells how they came in
and how they loved her dog and cats and doves.
It was the summer of 1987
and they came on bicycles
from a boat on the canal,
in the rain,
and stopped under her eaves
and she invited them in.
And the others listen,
having heard it before,
and shake their heads
about Americans riding bicycles in the rain.

How large it seemed to her
in the smallness of her kitchen
with its backless chairs and curtainless windows,
in the smallness of her village,
where foreigners come through,
sometimes in tanks and sometimes on bicycles,
sometimes to make war
and sometimes to come in out of the rain.

Years from now a boy will look at a snapshot.
His mother will say,
your Uncle Jim took this the day
we got caught in the rain,
and this old French lady,
see her in the shadows there,
invited us into her home.
The boy will smile at the picture,
but he can never believe
that in a village in France,
among old ladies gathered at the lavois,
there still is talk of how
their friend once saved the Americans from the rain.

Life in America

There's a line I want to use,
see?
in a poem I want to write,
okay?
Now don't groan or roll your eyes.
Give me a break.
I mean, hey, give it a chance
to grow on you,
okay?
It's a line I thought of,
watching some guys after a golf game
drinking in the clubhouse
and slapping cards on the table
and checking their watches and saying
like, you know, "oh hell,
about time to go home or my old lady will
give me a load of shit."
This line is about those guys
plus a lot of other people,
let me tell you,
people in loud dance places,
standing around the floor,
checking out the action,
if you know what I mean.
And people in bowling alleys,
okay?
yelling at the pins and each other.
This line,
and believe me, I wrote it myself,
I swear I never heard it before,
this line is about all those people I see
and not just those,

others,
at restaurants and ball games
and even at church.
It's a line about how they act
and in a way it's a line about America.
But hey, I don't want to get too heavy,
you know?
I just want to say this one little line
and let you take it from here,
okay?
Hey look, seriously, the line is
(are you ready for this?)
"living lives of boisterous desperation."
Lives of boisterous desperation.
How about that?
Not quiet desperation, like the other guy wrote
about another time and another place,
but boisterous desperation.
Get it?
Get it?
Sure you do.

The Story of the Beginning
of the End of the World

It was a time when many people had the answers.
Some sold the answers
to other people who came
on weekends to listen and
nod and hug each other and
sometimes scream and sometimes
take off their clothes and
always say "thank you for sharing."

Some sold the answers
in books about feeling better and
taking charge of your life and
walking a new path and
discovering many zones and spots
you never knew you had
in your head or on your body.

Some sold the answers
in church with quotations about
giving and receiving and
which one is always better and
warnings about finding the answers in
books or from false prophets
who abounded in times like these.

Some sold the answers
in business schools and in stock markets,
in union halls and in capitals of government
and, for those of lesser means,
in blind alleys and back stairways

and places where other people
wouldn't even think to look for the answers.

Leo

He threw water on my motorcycle's one sparkplug
so I wouldn't be able to leave him,
so I would have to stay,
his buddy,
and play in the back yard,
the only place he was allowed to go.

Early before anyone was up
he would fill a tumbler with tap water
then sneak out the front door
of his side of the duplex
and tiptoe to where the Harley 125 was chained
and pour a little puddle around the plug.

Later, late and frustrated,
drying the plug, grease on my hands,
I would yell at him

> *Goddammit, Leo, you're making me late*
> *I've got to go to school.*

and sometimes chase him and pretend
I was going to hit him.
But he would only repeat what he said
every morning of every day of every year
we lived in that duplex

> *You Leo's buddy*
> *Play with Leo now.*

Leo would stand,
his big droopy frame shutting out the light

from the back screen door,
and watch mother cook.

> *Rufe play with Leo?*

This breathing was noisy
and he sometimes drooled
and his eyes looked in different directions.
Mother would say "that big dumb thing
scares me and I wish they'd keep him
off the back porch."
and I would say "if he's so dumb
how does he know to ground out my sparkplug."

We knew his age and his mind's age
and we knew they'd didn't match,
but we didn't know anything else
except he was Italian
and his big family kept him there with them,
in the duplex,
and they had barbecues in the back yard
and drank beer and laughed with each other,
and that Leo played on the ground
with the other children
like a big pet, I thought.
And they all seemed happy enough.

I hadn't thought about Leo in years, of course,
until just the other day,
just after the tests were in,
just after the pediatrician
in his I am your friend voice
said something to us like,
"Well, he'll never go to Harvard Medical School,

but he'll be very functional
and will be able to do a lot of things."

Later, I wondered if that meant things like
ground out a sparkplug with a glass of water
or play the family pet
with children a third his age.

And I thought,
sometimes God makes you write things on the blackboard
a thousand times.

Distractions

It was a matter of distraction;
I could not hear my baby sons,
those struggling years ago,
in a trailer or an apartment
or old house where I thought
money was the problem
and did not want to be distracted
by the babbling of children.
Or it could have been the constrictions,
of a trailer, an apartment, an old house, a cockpit
or an office with two other people
and no way to stand out
but to put my head down and work
so hard I could not afford
to be constricted by children.

But this is not the same old cry of guilt,
the if-only-I-had-another-chance,
because after all these years
a chance came,
another son,
this time with me ready to listen.
But he is distracted,
something about constrictions in his brain
making him busy inside himself,
with so much to do
that he talks to himself
more than to me,
and every day I try to persuade him
to live in this world
and to let me know he's with me
if only from time to time.

Poet's Prayer

If I write another poem
let it be about love,
not the crazy love
we all start out writing about
but the love that keeps us sane,
the love that pain reveals
at a funeral
or when the doctor says what we don't want to hear;
the love that men won't talk about,
of work, of games, of one another;
the love of divorced people
when they find their way back to marriage;
the love of an old family place
when the generations gather there;
the love of old friends
who realize they're the only ones left;
and the love of children,
not only when they're smiling or sleeping
or clean or straight or strong or smart,
but when they are none of those things
and need more love than anyone can give,
and cannot even recognize the love they get.

Matters of the Heart

*(on the Lear, after learning of a
blocked coronary artery, April 20, 1980)*

What makes the heart stop?

> On the Lear the heart stops
> when the noise stops
> or the CAT* strikes.

What about the flatbed truck?

> Then too,
> Chigger trying to jump the ditch
> behind the road machine
> or hit it,
> on the way to Wolf River
> where the yellow water tried to suck me under.

And the motorcycle?

> Yes, I twisted the handlebar
> pushing myself at the heart's edge
> with the fear in seconds,
> spinning and tumbling on the muddy road.

What then of the cancer?

> It did not happen to me.

Didn't it?

> It was the heart, remember?

But it wasn't your heart connected to his cancer?

And to many things.

So what really makes the heart stop?

No one knows,
but I know this:
it practices and practices.

* *clear air turbulence*

Christmas in New York

Don't let Adeste Fideles near a tenor sax
or else
some gaunt music major
will beat it to death for tuition.
At Bloomie's the Salvation Army lady
carols on a baritone horn,
and a fey young man listens,
tiny jingle bells in a pierced ear.
On the church steps the Fifth Avenue Four
urge themselves onward
through the Saints,
from the music stamped
"Property of Juilliard,"
perfectly,
which is not how it is to be played.

Could I take my sax
and fake it through Christmas on a corner?
Not the music but the rest of it,
the youth
the cold
the needs
the hope
the feeling it hasn't passed me by,
or vice versa?

Homeless Saxophonist

I can tell from his riffs
he is not on Lexington Avenue,
leaning against Grand Central,
his fingers our only proof he's still alive.
We are here,
stepping around his feet,
pushing our way uptown,
his notes wild against the taxi horns.
But he is not playing where we are;
he is in another place,
a dark place small and crowded,
where people are smiling and shaking their heads
in that funny way real jazz fans have,
and there is a bass
and drums
and piano,
always with him, steady as dirt,
chords leading to just where he wants his sax to take him,
farther away still,
to a place he has not yet been
but will know the first time he feels it.

Why Men Fly

We sat around waiting
to see who had lit up the desert,
each of us with somebody
we did not want it to be,
burning out there,
coyotes and pack rats,
bright-eyed by the fire,
running jumping onto and around
rags of hot metal
scattered a mile,
nibbling perhaps at the odd chunks of meat.

All of us wondered the same thing
as each number landed,

>   *Apache four two is in*
>   *Apache one eight is in*

as each head-shaking, wet-suited man
came in counting the chairs,
checking each face for the missing one.

We did not know that melodrama
worked against us
until a Cajun boy hit his fist
on the table and sobbed,
"Why didn't they get out?"
And one of the instructors
hand-picked a bunch of us into another room
and said
"Anybody who can't take this without crying
better quit now."

Then as we tried variations on stony faced,
he said,
"After all, if flying were safe,
why the hell do it?"

Flying Safety Lesson

They said it was a lesson
about oxygen management,
then came a tape of radio talk,
an incident they called it,
involving a flight of four F-100s
from the States to Spain
with a stop in the Azores,
beginning with those voices you've heard
in the flying movies,

> "Check in, Red Four."
> "Roger."
> The Roger doesn't sound right,
> slurred,
> so the leader says "Oxygen check,"
> but by then it is already too late,
> and Red Four mumbles.

We knew why they wanted us to hear the tape,
something about fear,
about checking oxygen,
about things not to do
like starve our brains and dive into the sea,
old stuff we knew already.
But the mumble
made our necks tingle,
weeks later listening.

> The leader says, "Three, check out Red Four."
> Red Four says nothing,
> then Red Three shouts,
> "Pull up, Red Four, you're diving.
> Pull up, pull up."

We did not look at one another
but picked at our fingernails
or doodled or stared at the tape player.
Later we would discuss oxygen management
and safety checks
and all the routines that became so routine
between the Azores and Spain
that they didn't get done.

Then comes the radar controller's voice,
steady, commanding,
"Red Four, this is Racecar Radar,
turn heading one three five degrees,"
then scared,
"Sir . . . Red Four Sir . . . please
turn right . . . now . . . heading one four zero degrees."
Then Red Three drops the call sign,
"Bob, please listen to me,
pull up, level your wings,
look at me, wave, give me a sign,
say something."

Then the mumble,
trying hard we thought,
but too late the Flight Surgeon told the class,
"His brain was gone by that time, Gentlemen."

Now the tape plays a lot of silence.
Red Three says, "Bob, please pull up,
pull back on the stick, ease back on the stick."
And the radar man asks "Altitude?"
And Red Three says, "five thousand and descending,"
and the radar man says
"Red Four . . . sir . . . please turn right . . .
please pull up."

On Paying Attention

And Red Three says,
his voice breaking at the edges,
"Bob look at me, wave, pull up."
More silence.
"Too late, too late."
And the radar man gives the coordinates
and the tape shuts off.

I don't remember the words the instructors chose
to restate the obvious,
but I remember the lesson they never intended,
about how technology fails
and humanity is the only thing left,
which sometimes is not enough.

Examining the Wreckage

I am drawn to plane crashes.
I read about them,
every detail,
and try to figure out what happened
and what the pilot did wrong,
which is only a way of wondering what I would have done.

And of course I would have done it right,
have analyzed the problem,
the sputtering engine,
the heavy controls,
the failed generator,
and I would have gotten down okay,
and I would never would have flown in that weather,
and I would have watched for ice,
and I would have turned back,
and I would never have gone near that thunderstorm
or flown those mountains at night
or taken a single engine over water
or any of those dumb things
other pilots do every day.

But when I think about the pilot years
I remember things done wrong:
an aileron roll too close to the ground,
a foggy landing I should not have tried,
a thunderstorm full of hail
like the sound of a thousand hammers,
a failed drag chute, a blown tire
and a bomb under the wing.
All that without a crash.

At this point I should make a metaphor
about life and flying,
but flying is easier than life.
When a plane crashes,
I can go there and know
that I am not in the wreckage.

Jeopardy

I

How many times have I died?
At least once on the motorcycle,
with Jack Spencer on the back,
the unexpected car
and the boys on the bicycle
and nothing to do but skid and hope.
Or run off the road
by the Cadillac passing on the hill
outside Holly Springs.
And certainly in the F-86
over the cotton fields below Rabat
with Dickie on the radio

Jesus, Cowboy, pull up before you roll!

(Think of that,
of all the hoeing and picking,
of all the sun hot hours in cotton fields,
to hang my wing
and tumble into pieces
on some foreigner's cotton
ten thousand miles from my people's land.)

And in the fog at Wethersfield
in an Englishman's pasture
with sheep like gray boulders
in a wash of green
only a hundred yards from the runway
but far enough that all I could say
was Oh Shit.

And in the whistling silence
of a dead engine.
And in a thunderstorm
that rolled back and wrinkled the metal skin
like an old time cigarette paper.
And in a hundred things I didn't even know about.

II

There are courts of inquiry somewhere,
accident investigators piecing it together.
There are coroners,
there are undertakers trying to make me
look okay after all.
There are caskets shipped back
filled with rubber sacks
not nearly full enough.
There are honor guards clicking their heels
and firing rifles in country cemeteries.
There are proud mothers
and wet-eyed widows
and children with pictures for fathers.

III

But through all those deaths,
I am here,
still and again,
with at least one to go,
and the only thing changed
is the limb I am out on.

From
Love and Profit

Threads

Sometimes you just connect,
like that,
no big thing maybe
but something beyond the usual business stuff.
It comes and goes quickly
so you have to pay attention,
a change in the eyes
when you ask about the family,
a pain flickering behind the statistics
about a boy and a girl in school,
or about seeing them every other Sunday.
An older guy talks about his bride,
a little affectation after twenty-five years.
A hot-eyed achiever laughs before you want him to.
Someone tells about his wife's job
or why she quit working to stay home.
An old joker needs another laugh on the way
to retirement.
A woman says she spends a lot of her salary
on an au pair
and a good one is hard to find
but worth it because there's nothing more important
than the baby.
Listen.
In every office
you hear the threads
of love and joy and fear and guilt,
the cries for celebration and reassurance,
and somehow you know that connecting those threads
is what you are supposed to do
and business takes care of itself.

Seney's Gone

(In memory of Noel "Red" Seney, who taught me much)
With a stylistic nod to Donald Justice

There will be no more fun at the office.
Seney has died,
taking all his foolishness with him.
What will happen on a spring afternoon
when there is no Seney to lure us to the park
with a football, Frisbees, and a case of beer?
Will productivity rise
now that there is no silliness
to get in its way?

There will be no more fun at the office.
Seney has died,
taking all his foolishness with him.
How will we bear those meetings
to which Seney brought the only life,
a show-and-tell of some sort,
a joke perhaps or,
oh yes, a limerick
about ladies or men from places
that rhymed with an anatomic appendage?

It is easy to imagine Seney,
wherever he is,
still smoking and full of coffee,
organizing whatever parties they have there,
bringing angelic or demonic exuberance
to every new chorus
of "Chinamen never eat chili."

But there will be no more fun at the office.
Seney has died,
taking all his foolishness with him.
Where will we find the smiles
when things are late
and they're on our butts about the overtime,
when there's no way to get it all done
but we know we will
because we always do?
Where will we find the smiles?

Educated Fool

My grandmother used to talk about educated fools,
   All they do is sit
   at a desk,
   never do any work.
and I dreamed about how easy that would be,
sitting at a desk
instead of sweating in the sun and dirt,
instead of chopping cotton
or picking up potatoes or pulling weeds,
instead of fighting flies and sting worms
and wasps and sometimes a snake.
"Educated fool" didn't sound so bad,
all desks and telephones and secretaries,
eating in some air-cooled café
instead of trying to find a dark spot
of tree shade on the edge of a field,
with a sausage and biscuit and a jug of tea,
nobody to talk to but a mule or dog.

You know what comes next, of course.
You know I'm writing this at my desk,
on a Thursday,
and day after tomorrow
I'll put on bib overalls,
the neighbors thinking what an affectation,
and pull weeds for the composter,
and dig a place for a late row of greens,
most of them going to seed
instead of in the pot,
and tell myself what the hell,
I'll just want to dig the dirt
and watch the stuff grow,
an educated fool at last.

The Memo

It looked like any other memo,
corporate proper and neat,
with "to" and "from" and "cc" in order,
with margins straight
and text centered.
It came through inter-office mail
and appeared on our desks
just like any other memo.
It was the subject,
"Three of the greatest lies,"
that caught our eyes and made us read,

   1. You can eat anything with false teeth.
   2. I've never lied to you.
   3. We think we got it all.

Then it talked of CAT scans
and something called a
squamous-cell lung carcinoma,
strange words to find in our in-boxes.

Of course, it was not the first memo
about a change in plans,
nor was it even the first memo about fear.
But we want action memos,
you see,
we want memos
that leave us with something to do.
And this was a memo
about waiting.

The Leader

It was in the big paneled office,
on the sofa,
after a run at the Y,
that he said,
tears and sweat on his face,
"I've been such an asshole,"
then he bear-hugged me and said,
"You have to stay,
you're one of my people."
And I thought,
Okay if I can be this kind of businessman,
I'll be a businessman.

Then, somewhere along the way,
it got harder for him.
The skeptics, I think,
the loneliness.
He did not want to find any truth
in the old cliché
about isolation at the top,
but the gentle touch is more difficult
than the strong arm,
and a balancing act is more tiring
than you think.

But when I am patient
and look beyond the obvious,
it is still there,
something I am supposed to preserve.

I Am That Man

(In memory of Wayne Miller)

James Dickey once put on a dead man's helmet,
a man just killed in battle,
and Dickey's head filled with the dead man's last thoughts.

That poem came to me in a dead man's office
as I was arranging my stuff,
making my place in his place.
He faced one way, I would face another.
He liked blank walls and overhead lights,
I like paintings and plants for my eye
wherever it wanders.
He was quick with aphorisms
like "Plan your work and work your plan,"
and he knew that hard work
overcomes guile every time.
He believed in ladies and gentlemen
and starting on time
and being frugal with an expense account
("Treat the company's money like your own.")
And he was always one man at home
and the same man on the job.

Times change, of course, but I wonder,
if I wear this office like that dead soldier's helmet,
will they call me quaint some day?
Will my insights become sayings
that everybody thinks they've heard too often?
Will my truths become anachronisms
while another person measures my corner office?
Will I settle into this part of my business journey
like a man who sees times gathering

on both sides of every day,
who believes that things don't change
but that we talk about them differently?

Will I feel something gentle someday,
something calm come into the office,
and will I look out the window
and see children throwing clods in the river
and a mother gathering dry milkweed pods,
and will I know that, later,
a man will see them in a vase
on a table in a room
where he will read the Twenty-third Psalm before dinner,
home at last?
And will I know that I am that man?

The Meaning of Rich

When we said someone was rich,
we meant only one thing:
He never had to work another day in his life.
We did not know how much money it would take,
but as we entered the sweepstakes
and jingle contests
and shouted our quiz-show answers at the radio,
we figured sixty-four-thousand dollars would do just fine,
fifty dollars a week forever
and never work another day in our lives.

Money comes and goes,
and so does the meaning of rich,
but most of us retired before we learned
that nothing pays off
like having work to do.

Business Is Bad, I

How do you know when you've gone too far?
Maybe it's when someone asks,
"How are you?"
And you tell them how business is.
Maybe it's when business is bad
and it feels like a death in the family,
and you wonder how anybody can be happy,
the way you feel when you're on the way to a funeral
and find yourself wondering
why all those other people in the airport
are laughing and smiling as if no one had died.
Don't they know, don't they know?
Business is bad.

Maybe it's when you find yourself angry
in the midst of another, yet another,
birthday coffee or promotion party,
or when someone asks you to join in a baseball pool
or attend a fund-raising lunch,
or stop for an after-work drink
with the such-and-such department,
which is celebrating
another of those productivity milestones
we invent so we'll have something to celebrate.
"How do they have time for this crap?"
you ask yourself.
Don't they know, don't they know?
Business is bad.

On Paying Attention

Business Is Bad, II

He did not look well,
the paunch of too many receptions and dinners
at too many conferences
in too many hotels.
(Sometimes it's smiling too much
I think
and saying the same thing
over and over again,
a kind of social fatigue.)
And here he was,
eating and drinking,
this time with friends,
—never mind that we all work together,
that we talk about those same things—
in the home of another friend,
so I asked, "How are you doing?"
with an emphasis on the you.
And he shook his head
and frowned and tucked his chin
and swallowed like someone
whose mouth is dry
and said,
"That last profit forecast was rotten,
really a killer."

Leaving It All Behind

There were days when we still didn't get it,
that this wasn't like school or the military,
that we wouldn't graduate or get out
and leave it all behind.
We brought lunches in brown paper bags
and folded airplanes
to fly in the park.

We pitied the older guys
playing out their big-time businessman roles
as if most of them were not just some kind
of free-market bureaucrats.
Somehow we knew we'd do better
and we knew we'd be different,
without that need to cover our asses,
without that fear of failure.
We would give young guys like us
plenty of room to make us look good,
and we would ignore stupid policies and politics
and get rid of deadwood vice presidents
who wasted time and money and office space.
We would have the guts to take our money and run
before the job pushed us too hard
and the next title became too important,
before we found ourselves on airplanes every week
and in the office every weekend,
before our kids stopped caring if we were around,
and our wives drank too much
at too many ladies' luncheons
where they were going to have just a sherry
or one glass of wine,
before we got tired of smiling at every jerk

who might spend a dime with us,
before we ate every oversauced meal
and sniffed every cork and drank every bottle of wine,
before we went to every sunny resort
and heard every self-improvement speaker
and danced at every black-tie dinner
and applauded every chairman and program committee
and carried home every printed tote bag
and monogrammed vinyl notebook
and T-shirt,
and put every smiling group picture in a scrapbook.

Before all that,
we would get out.

Lights Flashing at O'Hare

Taxiing in on United at O'Hare
you see fire engines and an ambulance,
lights flashing,
and you think of snowy mornings
in a trailer somewhere in France,
near a runway of accelerating sounds,
loud but comforting in their consistency.
Then nothing,
and before you remember that silence
is not what you want to hear,
that fear born of something much older than airplanes
rises like a siren in your brain,
who who who who who?

In your briefcase is a calendar
filled for months to come,
time stretching like a chore
as far as you can turn the pages,
another week another year
to be played out in meetings and memos and trips.
Then, looking back toward the flashing lights,
ready by the runway,
you realize that out there somewhere
some poor son of a bitch
just wants to the next five minutes
to be over.

The Angler

He angled his way around New York,
always crossing diagonally,
never at the corners,
proud of saving a thousand miles of shoe leather
over his forty years of selling.

In the beginning, he called himself a drummer,
then a peddler with a shine,
and lately, a seller,
telling his drinking buddies, "We're all sellers,
no matter what you think you do."

He drummed and peddled and sold himself
into a nice club,
a house worth ten times what he paid
back when Greenwich was a sleepy town,
and a place on a golf course in Georgia.

He phones less now, writes fewer letters
than when he first made the move South
and called to check on us,
making sure we were keeping our noses clean
and the value of his stock high.
And he no longer invites us down for golf,
to sleep in the guest room and talk of old times,
realizing at last there are no angles into memory,
that we are remembered or forgotten
for things too late to change.

Still Chooglin' after All These Years

It was not the palm trees
or surf,
another paradise meeting
in a long list,
that brought the sudden shift.
But something put us together again
for the first time in a long time.
The music perhaps,
or David saying,
"These children don't choogle like we did,"
burnished our friendship
like an old and precious thing
stored away and not often remembered,
a treasure taken for granted,
sometimes handled carelessly
like those heirlooms you move in boxes
from house to house
and never seem to find a place for.
Something about the paradise
and the band
and the baby boomers dancing
and David saying, in his country-boy voice,
"Let's go show them young 'uns how to shake their booties,"
and we found ourselves in it again,
immersed and rising in the affection
of twenty years of giving it all we've got,
deadlines, planes, meetings,
celebrating a new product,
consoling ourselves about a failure,
fighting and losing touch,
feeling apart, betrayed, angry.
Yet in that wet night,

laughing at our potbellies and ancient dance steps,
we knew that what we've gone through
meant more than we ever thought it could.

What Personnel Handbooks Never Tell You

They leave a lot out of the personnel handbooks,
Dying, for instance.
You can find funeral leave
but you can't find dying.
You can't find what to do
when a guy you've worked with since you both were pups
looks you in the eye
and says something about hope and chemotherapy.
No phrases,
no triplicate forms,
no rating systems.
Seminars won't do it
and it's too late for a new policy on sabbaticals.

They don't tell you about eye contact
and how easily it slips away
when a woman who lost a breast
says, "They didn't get it all."
You can find essays on motivation
but the business schools
don't teach what the good manager says
to keep people taking up the slack
while someone steals a little more time
at the hospital.
There's no help from those tapes
you pop into the player
while you drive or jog.
They'd never get the voice right.

And this poem won't help either.
You just have to figure it out for yourself,
and don't ever expect to do it well.

On Firing a Salesman

It's like a little murder,
taking his life,
his reason for getting on the train,
his lunches at Christ Cella,
and his meetings in warm and sunny places
where they all gather,
these smiling men,
in sherbet slacks and blue blazers,
and talk about business
but never about prices,
never breaking that law
about the prices they charge.

But what about the prices they pay?
What about gray evenings in the bar car
and smoke-filled clothes and hair
and children already asleep
and wives who say
"You stink"
when they come to bed?
What about the promotions they don't get,
the good accounts they lose
to some kid MBA
because somebody thinks their energy is gone?

What about those times they see in a mirror
or the corner of their eye
some guy at the club shake his head
when they walk through the locker room
the way they shook their heads years ago
at an old duffer
whose handicap had grown along with his age?

And what about this morning,
the summons,
the closed door,
and somebody shaved and barbered and shined
fifteen years their junior
trying to put on a sad face
and saying he understands?

A murder with no funeral,
nothing but those quick steps outside the door,
those set jaws,
those confident smiles,
that young disregard for even the thought
of a salesman's mortality.

Cornered

Armed with a cup of coffee
and the requisite smile,
he sat cornered in this office at last
and crossed and uncrossed his legs
and asked if he could smoke
and said he didn't know about the money problem,
and I said, "It's your business
until you represent the company,"
and he said it was a misunderstanding,
and I asked about all the others,
and he said they were mistakes
and he would explain
and the company would not be liable,
and I said we'd heard it before.

He sucked the cigarette red and squinted
and said, "What do you want me to do?"
And I thought,
Oh God, I want you to quit,
to clear out, to take away this pain.
I want you to stand, shake my hand,
take early retirement, give it up,
find a job, land on your feet,
be happy. But I want you gone.
But I said, "What do you want to do?"
And he said, "I've been drinking a lot."
And I said, "I know."

I Find Myself Wishing

I find myself wishing I could be like Mr. Dithers
so I could jump up and dash down the hall
and into an office
and shout,
"Bumstead (or whatever the name is)
you blithering idiot, you're fired,
clean out your desk and be gone by five!"
What a luxury,
but it only happens in the comics.
There are the legalities, of course,
making the damned paper trail,
but that's not what stops me.
And it's not that firing someone
is, as the books say, my own failure.
No, I think it's knowing
that I will never be forgiven
even if I could apologize,
as in some cultures they apologize
to the game they are about to kill.
"Forgive me, please, I'm about to take your life.
You're fired."
Even that would be simpler than the real thing,
than now, sitting here,
waiting for the knock on my door.
Never mind the greater morality,
the justice of the group,
all those answers I know so well.
Let's bring it down to one and one,
a handshake,
some sentences,
what it takes to face the watering eyes,

the denial,
the disbelief,
the anger,
the fear,
the betrayal.

Resisting

There are days when the old ways seem easier.
To hell with consensus
and community building
and conflict resolution
and gentle persuasion.
Time to kick some ass,
turn some heads around,
get some action,
make this place move.
Time to stop asking questions
and give some orders.
Time to get things
ready for inspection.

It's an old urge,
the luxury of power,
the first temptation of bosshood,
and it comes like a bad temper
on a day when someone won't accept
the answer I gave,
and pushes again,
another five-minute meeting that eats up an hour,
another printout to prove a point not worth proving,
another ploy to protect someone's invisible turf,
another dance along that border
between debate and defiance.
I feel the anger flashing
and fight what I want to say,
all the top-sergeant stuff
like "Shape up or ship out,"
or "Tell it to the chaplain."
When I'm lucky,

the thought of those words
bouncing off the paneled walls
makes me smile.
When I'm not,
I take a very deep breath.

The Letdown

All the management books say
keep your expectations to yourself,
Give your employees goals
but not expectations.
All the child-care books say
the same thing.
But who do they think they're kidding,
those experts?
Haven't they ever had a child with promise,
a kid they just knew would do
everything they did,
and more?
Haven't they ever seen themselves
in the face and walk and hustle
of a young seller or engineer or manager,
and haven't they thought to themselves,
That's it,
that's what I'm looking for,
that's who I need,
the next one for the next big job?
And haven't they overlooked
the small things,
the should-have-seen-it-coming signs
that meant wait,
not ready yet,
too soon, slow down, hang on.
And didn't they think,
This is my guy
and he can't fail because he's as good
as I was,
and I'll help him over the rough spots,
and besides,

sometimes it's sink or swim in this business
and you can't know if you're ready
until you're right in the thick of it?

And have they never waited too long
to throw out the lifeline,
left only to watch the sinking
of their expectations?

Executive Health

Something happens,
a dizziness when you stand up,
a pain you never noticed before,
a heavy breath at the top of the stairs.
And you think about a friend in the hospital,
and wonder what's going to get you someday.
So you make another vow,
you buy a diet book
and new workout clothes
and a computerized treadmill
and meditation tapes,
and you renew the health-club membership
and get your racquet out of the closet
and inflate the tires on the bike
and walk three miles the very first day.

Then it's Monday,
and the broiled fish you were going to have
turns into pasta
and the dessert you'll always skip
becomes just sherbet,
and out of the office by five
means still there at seven.
On Tuesday you can't work out on an airliner,
and who in his right mind jogs
after dark in a strange city?
And the tapes you play for stress
put you to sleep at the wrong time,
so you lie awake later,
listening to the horns and the garbage trucks
and the sound of your own breathing,
and vow to make another start this weekend.

On Paying Attention

Listening and Learning

There was a time I listened
to the men at the store,
thinking I could learn about farming
as they came dusty from the fields
in bib overalls and long-sleeved shirts,
their hands and faces dark red
save a white band where their straw hats sat.
They kicked their boots on the ground,
red clay dust rising to their knees,
and shook their heads as they came in the door.
Always shook their heads and met the eyes
of other farmers who shook their heads
and stood at the co-cola boxes
with a Coke or a Dr. Pepper or RC.
I listened about the weather
and the government
and the prices,
all of it turned against them.

Now, I watch businessmen
stretch and squeeze time on planes
and in offices,
measuring their days by meetings and phone calls,
then gather in clubs
and bars and restaurants
and shake their heads and talk and talk,
about inflation and disinflation,
about the government and the deficit
and the margins
and the share fights.

After a while, it sounds the same,
farmers and businessmen,
and what I hear
is how hard it is
for them to say how much they love it.

Self-made?

He called himself a self-made man,
and his colleagues agreed.
"The kind of man who built this country,"
they said,
"Never asked anybody for help."
"Never took a dime he didn't earn."
"Made it on his own."
And so forth.

But can that really be,
the self-made somebody?
How many times do we ask for help
without ever using the words?
How much are we paid
before we're good enough to earn
the dimes we take?
And can we climb the ladder alone,
or do some of us just never notice
those lifts and boosts
along the way?

Recessions

Why do we keep on keeping on,
in the midst of such pressure,
when business is no good for no reason,
when everything done right turns out wrong,
when the Fed does something
and interest rates do something
and somebody's notion of consumer confidence does something
and the dogs won't eat the dog food?

What keeps us working late at night
and going back every morning,
living on coffee and waiting for things to bottom out,
crunching numbers as if some answer
lay buried in a computer
and not out among the people who
suddenly and for no reason
are leaving their money in their pockets
and the products on the shelves?

Why don't we just say screw it
instead of trying again,
instead of meandering into somebody's office
with half an idea,
hoping he'll have the other half,
hoping what sometimes happens will happen,
that thing, that click, that moment
when two or three of us
gathered together or hanging out
get hit by something we've never tried
but know we can make work the first time?

Could that be it,
that we do all the dull stuff
just for those times
when a revelation rises among us
like something borning,
a new life, another hope,
like something not visible catching the sun,
like a prayer answered?

How It Was

They'll never know how it was,
the younger guys,
to bust our asses for a six-hundred-dollar raise
and a title change
and twice as much work.
They'll never bring lunch in a brown bag
or sneak to Lemo's
for a frosty beer when it was ninety-five degrees,
and the cheap bastards wouldn't spring
for air conditioning,
and our pants stuck to the chair
and we thought we should get paid
for extra dry-cleaning.

Now everything is easy,
and they'll never understand,
the younger guys,
about changing things
and how long it took
to wait the old guys out.

Retirement Party

They all come,
even the ones who think
he was a pain in the neck.
They come and talk
about how he will be missed,
most of them never noticing he was there.
They come for themselves,
like going to a funeral
out of the fear of being buried alone someday.

They line up for coffee
and punch and cookies,
there being no official alcohol on the premises.
They read telegrams from old customers and old vendors
and old office buddies long retired.
They give him the right gift,
the rod and reel
or the camp stove
or the camera
or the round-trip ticket to somewhere,
bought with the fives and ones and quarters
from the manila envelope that has
in his last month
made its way all around the company.

He is moved by the attention,
by the feeling he is loved
and will be missed
and things won't be the same without him,
and he says some words
about how he will never forget any of them.

He introduces his family, who came halfway across the country
just for the occasion,
then everybody drifts toward their offices
saying goodbye with things like
"You lucky bastard,"
and "You don't even have to get up tomorrow,"
and "Stay in touch,"
and "Come visit,"
and other words of comfort for times like these.

Romantic Revelations

My friend has an infallible rule
for spotting a romance in the office,
a rule true and proven over the years,
accurate in direct proportion
to how hard the lovers try to hide.
My friend calls it the Law of Romantic Revelation,
and it goes like this:

> *If you think they're doing it,*
> *they're doing it.*

Sounds silly but it's damn near perfect
if you have any power of observation at all.
If for instance a very solid citizen,
say a forty-five-year-old guy,
stops getting a haircut every other week,
and as the hair begins to hide his ears and collar,
you notice the gray ones are gone,
or if he shows up in an Italian blazer,
unvented,
with notched lapels,
watch out.
Next thing you know he's collecting wine
or original prints.
Then one day you're in a meeting
on personnel policy
and find he has become a feminist
since the last meeting,
or you notice in the corner of his office
a new Land's End canvas bag
for his running shoes and designer sweats
and one of those Fit at Fifty
posters on the wall.
You have but to keep your eyes open

and the object of his affectations
will come into focus
and the Law of Romantic Revelation
will unveil its infallibility once again.

A Homeless Poem

I don't want to hear any of those poems
about how we are all homeless,
drifting on this planet, alone
in a cold and dark universe.
Baloney.
I want to hear a poem
about how some of us are homeless
and we step over and around them
and wish somebody would do something
that wouldn't raise taxes.
I want to hear a poem about
children in an abandoned car
scared in the night
that what has happened will happen again.
I want to hear a poem
about nice neighborhoods up in arms
because squatters have moved into the park
and are shitting under the shrubbery.
Spare me those lines
about how alienated we are,
how powerless,
how apart and how isolated;
spare me please all those phrases
of comparative misery
we use at cocktail parties
on the way to the therapist.
Write me instead a stanza of despair.
Make me feel the pain
when a baby's mother breaks its legs
and thinks she's only playing.
Make me vomit at the thought
of what a child has to eat.

Fill me with that insane warmth
an infant feels sucking milk
from an addict mother's breast.
And make my heart roar
with the screams and sobs and moans
rising from the streets
and storefronts and overpasses
and bridges and park benches and slum rubble
and garbage dumps and junkyards
all over this land of plenty.

From
Life & Work
(1994)

Downsizing

Too many times has a death message
come late at night
for me not to fill with fear
when the telephone pulls me awake.

And when I hear the voice,
I know the news is bad.
"How can they just eliminate my job like that?"
I don't know.
"After all these years?"
I don't know.

We talk a long time
about when we were younger
and everything was uncertain but full of promise,
thinking then that money was the goal
and the job was just something we did.

But now we know the truth.
"I can get by financially, I guess,
but that's not the point.
It's the work."
"Yes."

Then at this pause,
from the silence on the end of the phone,
comes at last that same sound
of other late-night phone calls,
grief, loss, disconnection,
and yet something else,
something like rejection,
but even more than that,

as if a whole life of work
has been without worth,
so insignificant that it can be legislated away,
the way some governments
simply erase all traces
of a person's life and work,
as if he had never existed.

The phone fills with silence.
Finally, as after those other death messages,
there is nothing left to say
except the trivial.
My old colleague apologizes for waking me
and trusts that I won't be tired in the morning
and fears I have been upset
and knows there is nothing I can do
and hopes we can get together soon
and appreciates my support
and may call me for a reference
and wishes my family well.

Death Message

I was in the big strategic planning meeting,
of all places,
the once a year pull out all the stops
and try to convince everyone including ourselves
that we know what tomorrow will bring
and if it brings something different
we will be ready meeting,
when my secretary, eyes down and head shaking,
handed me the note:
"They want you at the hospital . . . Red's failing fast."

It does not work to say
that we are all dying
and it is simply a question of when;
it does not make death more natural
nor does it make us less surprised
even when we are expecting it.

"Any day now," we had been saying,
yet it seemed to me Red's last prank,
dying in the middle
of a strategic planning meeting,
knowing I would pick up and leave
and the planning department's beautiful schedule
would be forever out of whack
because death is just not a contingency
they know how to plan for.

His lung had collapsed by the time I arrived
but over the respirator mask
his eyes widened and he squeezed my hand
with more strength than he could spare.

His brother-in-law said,
"Hell, he's gone, he's not here now"
even though the breathing had not stopped.
And I thought of meetings and trips and parties,
of where he started and how far he came
from a tiny town in Iowa to a big publishing company
and how much he brought with him,
old-fashioned stuff and corny as hell,
yet something we all came to depend on
and would never be able to replace.

The next morning on my desk,
another note from my secretary:
"They finished the meeting without you."
And I thought,
it won't be the last time.

Obsolete

"I just can't talk to them anymore.
They're kids, they don't listen."
It was the last thing he could say,
all that remained from a life of selling
which stretched from a smile and a shine
to a couple of martinis,
a flip chart,
and enough orders to send the kids to college.
It's the face you sell, he had thought,
shaving each morning,
and he could always go out and sell it
to anybody regardless of the product.
And he knew he'd never lose his gift of gab,
from his mother's Irish side,
but it never crossed his mind
that just when things ought to ease off,
when he should be able
to coast onto retirement,
he would find himself among people
who thought everything he said
sounded like some lost language,
quaint but without meaning for them.

Debts and Payments

World War II was mostly movies to me,
certainly not headlines,
because I did not read the papers then.
Even the war news came as newsreels
in the movie houses,
so the planes and tanks and soldiers
all were bigger than life,
heroic beyond my imagination,
and we would rush home and play war
shooting and pretending we were hit,
contorting our faces in agony
but always managing to toss one last grenade,
littering our neighborhood with dead nazis and japs.
After the war soldiers returned
with medals and money and war brides.
And stories.
Slowly we learned that the storytellers
had not seen much combat
and that the quiet ones had the real stories
but they were not telling.

Years later, in the 1980s, I worked with a man,
short, a bit pudgy, quiet,
a man of modest ambition
who did a mechanical job competently
but with obvious reluctance to even be noticed
much less be promoted into more responsibility.
He was in my operating group,
which means I was his big boss,
and in reviewing a staffing plan,
I was told it was not he who was judged extraneous
to the new way of doing things,

it was his job.
I was about to okay the plan
when the quiet man's supervisor
said, "This is not exactly relevant,
but I wasn't sure you knew
that he commanded one of the first tanks to reach
the Rhine . . . saw a lot of action."

No, it was not relevant
to our new way of doing things,
but I could think only of what pain,
what real contortion of face and body,
what smells and sounds,
what fear
he must have witnessed
while I was playing war in the grass.

"We'll wait," I said, to reactions
clearly divided by generations.
"Some things just cost a little extra."
Other things are never fully paid.

A Long Way to Drive

Some days I wish I had
a jug of coffee and a long way to drive,
down some blacktop
in the middle of nowhere,
headed to somewhere
but in no hurry.
When the tank moved toward empty,
I'd stop,
or when my eyes fell on some smoky shack
with a pile of hickory wood outside
and an RC COLA sign
with BAR-B-Q on it,
I'd pull in,
and when my dust cloud settled,
I'd decide on beans or slaw,
and that would be it,
my big decision of the day.

But I hear somewhere in the back of my head
a country boy saying, "Horseshit,
anybody believe that, take out a eyeball."
I hear him talking about how
I used to drive blacktop roads,
moaning every mile of the way
about making a lot of money someday
and working in an office
and traveling anywhere
and having a big car
and knowing a lot of important people.
"In the high cotton," I'd say,
"up among the high rafter bats."

Everything they ever said was true
about what money can't buy,
but they never said it's easier
to believe what money can't buy
after you have some money
you can't buy it with.

Questions

As kids we were told
at some point in the climb
the question would become
"How much money do you want
and what are you willing to do for it?"
A clichéd question, of course,
and as it turned out after thirty years in business,
one I've never heard asked
of anyone anywhere
except in the movies and on TV.
In our early days,
sometimes we asked it of ourselves
as if we had a choice
other than to keep climbing or quit,
not how much money,
but money or no money.

There is the myth,
on campus or in the church
or the union halls
or the congress or the military
or the civil service,
everywhere except in business,
that we can pull back,
let up, slow down, ease off,
that all we have to do
is just decide to take less money.
It is our desire for money,
they think,
that keeps us at the office or on the road
twelve hours a day
six days out of seven.

Listen,
Most of us do our jobs
because we love to do our jobs
and we know only one way to do our jobs.
Take it or leave it.
Yes, the money has its place
in our hierarchy of needs,
as they say,
sometimes a symbol of praise,
sometimes a measure of worth,
sometimes a way to buy time;
as for the questions,
they are always lying there somewhere,
often just below the surface,
but they are never about money.

Of Corporations and Communion

Adapted for my friends at
Murdoch Magazines, Sydney, Australia

In a way,
the good people are still with us,
all those you can name
plus many you never knew.
They are part of this celebration
which as we know
is not about careers and accomplishments
but about life itself,
life and the two things that keep us living,
relationships and work,
the people we love and the things we love to do.
So, many of those who have gone before
are here,
and in a way,
so are the ones who are still to come,
even those not yet born.
"How can that be?" you ask.
Consider this:
Life and work and love in any setting,
even a corporation,
can be acts of communion
transcending all of us who pass through,
with our only hope being
that when we retire or take our leave,
we have left something of ourselves,
enough that part of us will be there always.
"And how do we do that?" you ask.
Listen.
Work, those things we have set ourselves to do,
is like everything else in life,

and our chance for immortality
comes only through what we have done
to help other people.
Some of us succeed, some of us don't.

If in a business enterprise we could,
as in the church, attach special spiritual significance
to those who succeed,
if we could build shrines or dedicate holy places,
if we could but call them
teacher or master prophet or saint,
there might be words available,
a vocabulary of praise we could use
to commemorate what they have done.
But we are reduced to this:
They will always be here.

And so, we pray,
may we all.

Getting through the Stack

There was a sales manager in Chicago
who would sit at his dining table
and color maps,
a different color for each territory,
then he would take them to the office,
where they would become the marching orders
for his platoon of salespeople.
One time when the children in school
were telling what their fathers did,
his daughter said, "He colors maps."
He quit after that,
saying that the measure of any job
should be how a child describes it,
moved west and bought a little newspaper,
something he could hold in his hands every week.

It's easy for me to understand why he quit,
as I sit at my desk early
before anyone else is in,
moving the paperwork
carefully, thoughtfully, deliberately
from my IN box
across the desk where I sign
or initial or write notes in the margins,
to my OUT box,
one stack getting smaller, the other larger,
and I can measure the change,
that simple act satisfying me
more than anything I will do all day.
It is the most tangible
yet the least of what I am to do.

Big News

The game is won by those
who learn the news before everyone else.
The game has no name
but it is pursued seriously
and is taken as a measure
of a person's involvement in "the industry."
(It reminds me of nothing so much
as small-town gossip
with each industry a different small town.)
One day in New York
our industry was abuzz.
One of our competitor companies was shutting down,
selling its properties one by one.
All morning in our halls nothing but speculation
about people and products
and where they would go.
All but lost was the news
that one of our secretaries,
unmarried and no doubt scared,
had decided to have the baby
and had chosen this day
to let us in on it.
It would have been big news for our group
on any other day,
but today the game was on
and news like that gets no points.

On Trying to Write a Note to an Employee
Whose Baby Died of SIDS

I have written a million little notes,
by hand on these personal pads,
about new jobs and promotions and raises,
about babies born,
about triumphs of all kinds
from college degrees to bowling trophies.
And I have written, of course,
about deaths in the family.
But there are times
when I know that anything I say will fall short,
when any word I choose will be wrong.

I think now of my little boy
so few years ago in his crib
and how I would check him in the night,
fearful as ever that good things
live always in peril,
cupping my hand around his head,
watching for the breaths
which it seemed to me
could so easily stop,
and I think of how it would have felt
to wait for a breath
that did not come again.

Words will never do,
and even my tears on this blank sheet
will have no meaning for her.

Freedom

They were putting a glass skin on the building,
a giant one-way mirror
behind which we in our offices
could watch the world
but nobody out there could watch us.
It was to save energy, they said,
so bear with the noise
and the distraction of men hanging outside our windows.
We got so used to it
we would tuck in our shirttails
or rearrange our underwear
or do those other private little things
people do when they think no one is watching.
One day, a different movement, a fluttering
pulled me to the window.
There, on the sill, a pigeon.
It tried to fly through the one-way mirror
but was driven upward by the glass,
then sideways
from one office windowsill to another.
It would disappear from my view and return,
then finally, along with it, came people
following the pigeon from office to office,
some shooing it with their hands
and encouraging it with words,
"Fly down. Down. Dive. It's closed at the top,"
as if they could explain the logic
of the construction to the pigeon.

One man, a literary sort,
began to talk about it as a metaphor.
"The sun and sky and freedom are an illusion.

He can't get to them the obvious way."
The man was right, of course,
but knowing how not to get there
was not enough for the pigeon
who with each try became weaker
until it fluttered to the sill below
and the one below
and out of sight.

I like to think
that when it fell at last
below where the men were working
and realized it had stumbled onto freedom,
it still had the strength
to make another start.

Retirement

It is early.
Six-thirty.
The building is quiet.
I came in to write letters
and to pack.
Soon the place will come to life,
as it always does,
with the rush of people working.

These days, though, it's the smaller, slower things
I notice:
the droning of fans and compressors,
keeping us warm or cool,
the buzz of fluorescent lights,
the burble of the big percolator
and the smell of coffee,
the talk of the secretaries outside my door,
or a sudden laugh halfway down the hall.

As the time here grows shorter,
I find myself thinking of other times
when I could not wait for the day, or the week,
to be over,
the times I strained toward Christmas or a vacation,
an exquisite few days away from it all.
I think of meetings that would never end,
of hours stuck on a taxiway,
airliners lined up as far as I could see,
of those eternal minutes right before someone
was to come into my office
to be fired.

I understand now why every writer who ever lived
wrote about time and its paradoxes.
And everything they ever said
about how fast time passes is true.
But they never told us how many slow days
we would have to endure
before we realized how fast they had gone.

Corporate Marriage

She was more like his oldest daughter
though I doubt even a daughter
would have taken those scoldings
or settled for an allowance
or accepted a last will and testament
that guaranteed his immortality
by controlling the money from the grave,
as if assigning his financial ghost
to make sure that she in her girlish ways
would not squander the hard-earned estate.

He thought she had it made,
a good life,
more than her parents ever expected her to have
and all she had to do was marry him,
give him children,
entertain his guests,
and look the right part
in the right place
at the right time.
Not such a bad assignment
in the scheme of things, he thought.

When she moved out her explanation was,
as he would have expected, foolish:
"I'm the one with the master's degree after all."
It was not rational enough
for him to take apart,
listing and examining each element
in his reliable decision-tree method,
so he finally concluded that

"If a problem is not rational
what am I supposed to do about it?"

This is an old story,
a cliché even,
about the failed marriage of a corporate exec.
You've heard it all before
and you know what comes next,
the shock of friends
and puzzlement of the grown children,
attempts to keep it out of the papers,
a settlement that would be
referred to ever after as generous,
and plays and replays at the clubs
and on the golf courses,
those conversations ending always with the hope
that perhaps with a little luck
time will take care of it,
and people can get back to business.

The Sexual Revolution

My little part of the sexual revolution
had its start in a dark and crowded bar
where all the up-and-coming businessmen
met the women who came to meet
the up-and-coming businessmen.
La Boucherie it was called,
with butcher block tables and steaks
(the meat market pun lost on no one),
a kind of Shangri La for men
who did not want to go home
to all those obligations
that robbed them of their manhood,
who felt free among the people
of La Boucherie,
the turtlenecked, blazered, and blow-dried real estate guys,
the miniskirted Delta stewardesses,
tan from their San Juan layovers
(always emphasizing the lay in layovers).
We were Strangers in the Night,
Transformed by Witchcraft,
and carried Up Up and Away
in one another's Beautiful Balloons,
coming down much later
in our swamp of lies and anger,
our resolutions and promises lasting
only until the next evening at five.

The Summer of 1992

In my flowers, an unusual visitor,
a goldfinch eating seeds
from a fading stand of coreopsis,
gold and black on gold and black.

Last month, a storm
blew my young corn to the ground.
Now the stalks are tasseling
but there are no silks
and without them the pollen
is just another broken promise.

In the newspaper, a famine
in Somalia and killing in Yugoslavia
and South Africa and Uzbekistan,
places where hope seems to bear no fruit
after a season of such expectation.

This morning, I cut leaves and suckers
from the tomatoes which
for no reason I understand
have overgrown with foliage
and now need a new surge of life
and sunshine before it is too late.

It has been a strange summer.
All the sure signs are unreliable.
Everything is late in ripening.
There seems nothing to do,
yet waiting is not enough.

The Evidence

For Mark W. Bennett, U.S. Magistrate Judge,
on the occasion of his swearing in

Learned people speak learned words,
crowding sentences with jargon and acronym,
the assembled evidence
of a path taken toward this time and place.

I come with a different testimony,
not of law but of love,
of a parallel path
toward this same time and place.

Yet I sit in this courtroom with no hard evidence,
no sworn statements,
no pleadings,
no depositions.
All the evidence is soft,
but, may it please the court,
that is the power of it.

On the Concorde
3/26/90, N.Y.–Paris

Thirty years ago
when few had done it
and doing it was something rare,
we wore in our lapels
the emblem of the Machbusters' Club,
that loose collection of fighter pilots
who in straight-down dives
had entered the exclusive world
beyond the speed of sound.
We swaggered,
we of the bent wing airplanes,
the Sabre jet boys,
the ones with caps worn low
on the bridge of our nose,
the ones with top buttons unbuttoned,
uniforms no longer suited for the new domain.

How primitive it seems,
sitting now in a business suit,
with my wife who at mach one point seven oh,
is looking at a map of Paris,
who did not notice when we slipped
through what was once called
the barrier.
And I think, for the first time
in three decades,
"I'm going the fastest I've ever gone,"
then close my eyes for a nap.

On Paying Attention

On Hearing the Ukrainian Children Sing in Church

Des Moines, Iowa, January 24, 1993

Twenty years before these children were born,
I fought the Cold War
at a small air base in Germany
where I spent the days studying maps,
checking the plane and the bomb,
then practicing,
practicing in my head,
always ready,
even eager,
for the call,
and where I spent the nights dressed
in everything but my boots,
waiting for the siren
that would send me running
to be in the air in five minutes,
to use all my skills
to fly at the speed of sound
to a place I had never been
and had seen only in photographs,
to drop my bomb,
and if I did my job well,
to kill perhaps the parents-to-be
of these very children.

Oh what music the world would have missed.

Thinking about Sarah

We know when to celebrate, but
when do we start grieving?
Some say, "As soon as we know
life is ending."
Yet we know that life
is always ending,
and do not grieve every day;
it would be too much
even for a born griever like me.
So years ago we made an agreement with ourselves:
We wait for a doctor to give us the signal,
then we begin to grieve.

But now there's a new question:
What about those tiny lives,
the new ones measured by the ounce
and the minute,
the ones that leave us
not knowing if our tears
are in celebration or in mourning?

With every report from the hospital
I am smiling and grieving,
smiling and grieving.

Vacation Poem

How the thing with Ronald
pushes through, as soon as we relax,
away on a vacation,
alone, quiet.
It comes without form
but a presence nonetheless.
Heavy. Intruding. Calling
us away from our pleasure
as if pleasure is no longer allowed,
as if we must always be aware,
constantly dealing with
this thing,
this fear,
this future.

Ordinary Children

I get tired of seeing competent children,
with facile fingers writing,
tying shoes, buttoning shirts, zipping jackets,
playing complicated games
on computers,
or throwing balls at bats
and in baskets.
I get tired of those agile little bodies
on bicycles or skateboards
shifting their weight and balancing,
jumping curbs or dodging one another,
the way competent children do ordinary things.
They are the daily reminders,
these ordinary children of other parents,
and I get tired of being reminded.

Fellow Travelers

A boy stutters to me,
his eyes askew behind thick glasses,
about airplanes and coming home from Florida,
about the weather and cars
and anything else that crosses his mind
in these few minutes,
and I recognize him instantaneously,
and want to rush to his parents
and take their hands and,
through the distress and fatigue
they feel changing planes at O'Hare
with this strange and unpredictable child,
cry Yes Yes I know I know
and Don't despair
and We're all in this together
and Despite everything,
it's worth it.

A Wedding Poem at 30,000 Feet

Thinking about you
and how your lives have blossomed and faded
and blossomed again
with moments of love lost and found
on the way finally
to one single day in October,
I wonder what words can possibly celebrate
such a journey.
I have no vocabulary,
I give up.
There are plenty of poems
and I will choose someone else's,
a fine poem, a classic perhaps.

Then, floating in the light turbulence of a clear sky
(a sign that there can be turbulence
even in the clearest conditions),
I look over at Sally
dozing with that serenity she carries
from day into night,
from waking into sleeping and back again,
a calm I can only imagine
but which I know bears me through each day.
And I am moved one more time to find the words,
to bring up from somewhere a sense,
even a hint,
of what it is to understand at last
how the love of one person can deliver us
into a life we didn't even know we believed in.
Not a life without pain or anger or hurt or disappointment;
to the contrary, a life with all of that,

and yet,
a life without despair.

Is this all I can write for you
on this happy day,
not a poem of blessing
for a love of excitement and pleasure and comfort,
but instead for a love that promises only
that you are delivered forever from despair?
Yes, my friends, yes.
I can do no more,
for this is love's only guarantee.

From
Confessions of an
Accidental
Businessman
(1996)

Man of the House

The first scar came when the boy jumped a barbed wire fence
    on the way to school.
When the wire tore into the flesh of his calf it was not the pain
    that made him cry but the anger that this would not have
    happened if his mother had let him walk the drainage ditch
    to school.
"If there's a flood, you will drown," she had said which was
    dumb as hell since it wasn't about to rain but she had been
    crying again so he had not argued.
His third grade teacher sent him home because he was tracking
    blood and she said he needed stitches. She knew his
    mother would be looking for a job but his teacher sent
    him home anyway, his shoe squishing blood at every step.
The banty rooster was gone, and the hens, two or three days,
    so he was not all that surprised when Mickey did not come
    at his whistle. Still, he was too heartbroken not to cry.
His pants were ruined maybe, torn, bloody, but he put them
    in the tub to soak then he washed his leg, poured coal oil
    on a rag and pressed it onto the gash.
Damn it hurt.
The boy wondered why he had miscalculated, had missed
    the jump, but he had known as he left the ground that he
    would not be high enough. He remembered thinking, that
    instant in the air, he should have just walked the ditch.
But he was trying to be a man for his mother as she had told
    him he would now have to be even though he knew she
    still wanted him to be a child.
He had liked the idea of being the man of the house but after
    three weeks it was not working out that way.
The man of the house would have known about the bantys and
    would not have let them be taken away, and the man of the
    house would have his dog to call when he came home.

The boy did not understand all that had happened but he knew
that many things were happening without his knowing why.
He knew he had not seen his father since the night they were
going on a camping trip, were walking out the driveway to
where his father had said the car was parked and loaded,
and his mother came screaming, "No you don't, no you
don't. You're not taking him with you."
The boy had looked out to the street where the car sat idling.
He wanted to go but his mother, pushing past his father,
grabbed his hand and pulled him back. His father
grabbed the other hand, and they stood that way for a
while, his mother crying, his father saying, "Come on, son,
don't you want to go camping with Dad?" Then his mother
saying, "You are not taking him from this house. I know
what you're planning to do. For God's sake, leave me
somebody who loves me." She was sobbing.
The boy felt his father's hand slip away like someone falling.
Then the car was leaving and his father was gone.
The boy knew he could not take his father's place in this house.
He could not even try.
Pulling the blood and coal oil soaked rag from his leg and tying
a towel around it, he decided that all he could do now was
try not to cry.
Later he told his mother it was her fault he had torn his leg.
She seemed to accept this verdict and he could tell she
was choking on her tears again.
The next day, and every day after that, without asking anyone,
he walked the drainage ditch to school.
As for the torn leg it healed finally, without stitches,
and that scar is hardly visible today.

At the Air Aces Museum
Falcon Field, Arizona, March 1995

After I find the photograph,
a pilot younger than I ever was
standing one foot in the cockpit, one on the wing,
smiling with six fingers in the air,
one for each enemy plane he had shot down
on that single mission when he dove into
a swarm of Messerschmidts,
I ask the office lady for his address,
eager to let her know the connection:
"He was my old squadron commander,
William T. Whisner, triple ace in Europe,
ace in Korea, one of six aces of both wars,
Bendix trophy winner, the Whiz Kid they called him,
I flew with him in the Cold War."
She pulls out a book and runs her finger down a column.
"He died in 1989," she says
and tells me the circumstances,
about how the Whiz Kid, safely retired,
was caught by a surprise attack in peacetime.

In that last dogfight of my imagination
I can see him twisting, turning,
using all his old tricks to outrun them,
but he has lost his edge,
gotten rusty in the later years,
and one dives, turning inside him
and will not be shaken,
then as the Whiz Kid slows,
the killer gets just enough lead,
"An allergic reaction," the Aces Museum lady said.

Think of that,
of all the flying things that tried to do him harm,
Messerschmidts, MIGs, Fokkers,
and the Whiz Kid is shot down by a damned yellow jacket.

From
Looking Around for God
(2007)

Egypt (3/31/90)
By Sally Pederson

We stopped at the Cairo Carpet School,
a dozen ladies looking for a bargain.
Unsuspecting.
The schoolmaster spoke with pride,
"The children come to us at five or six years old.
We like to get them young so they can
learn the trade quickly.
They work for four hours with a break after two.
And we give them a free meal every day."
He smiled.

They sit there in a row
on low benches in front of looms,
tying colored threads to match the paper
pattern hanging before them.
Their tiny fingers move deftly, machine-like,
over, under, looping and
knotting the silk string.
There's a lump in my throat.
Upstairs in the showroom we see
the magic silk carpets change colors
before our eyes
when the salesman turns them
side to side.
"Handmade. Very good price."

But standing downstairs, among the children
I cannot help but think of my six-year-old
who cannot tie his shoes
and would not be so lucky
as these children

if his soul had been born
to an Egyptian child.

Meditation

All I really know about life I can say
in a few lines:
In April the small green things
rise through the black Iowa soil
whether we're ready or not.
The Carolina wren makes her nest
in the little redwood house
my son built from a kit.
Daffodils, tulips, irises get the attention as usual
while purslane, pig weed, and lamb's quarters
quietly take over a place
while no one is watching.

In June the corn shoots
etch long green lines
across the dark loamy fields,
and the greenest of all green grasses
crowd into the ditches and line the roads.
In August the early bloomers
begin to burn themselves out,
but in September the late yellows appear,
luring the bumblebees and yellow jackets
into a frenzy of pollination.

You already know about October,
the color, the last burst of extravagant life.
And then all at once it seems
everything retreats, pulls into itself, rests,
and prepares for the inevitable resurrection.

From *Looking Around for God*   247

The Resurrection

For Jim Gillion, Easter Sunday, 1994

This story is about a little girl
who died on Easter Sunday
and about her father who could no longer whistle.
Everyone knew at once,
the family, the neighbors,
that life would never be the same
without the little girl,
but it took a while for everyone to realize
that life would never be the same
without the father's whistle.
No one tried to talk him into it
because they understood the whistle
was somehow with the little girl,
gone, it seemed, forever.

Nobody knew what happened that day at the plant,
or if anything did,
but even before he arrived home
a neighbor lady called to say
how much it meant to hear the whistle.
"Your father has started whistling again,"
the mother told her son,
who then carried the father's tune in his heart
until one Easter Sunday
many years later and many miles away,
in a sermon of resurrection,
the son was able at last to tell this story,
and to whistle.

And the spirit of his father was released
as a blessing to all who heard it.

Questions for a Seventeen-year Cicada

Note: The Seventeen-year Cicada, upon hatching, drops to the ground and burrows into the earth where it stays as a larva for seventeen years, after which it makes its way to the surface, breaks open its shell, dries its wings, and flies into the trees. It remains there for a few weeks, feeding and singing its mating song incessantly throughout the day. Then it mates and lays its eggs under the bark of branches. The eggs hatch and the cycle begins again.

Were you surprised,
after waiting all those years,
to emerge still helpless
and struggling to find your wings
in this world
of birds with hungry beaks
and children with cruel fingers,
before you could fly up into the bliss
you had dreamed about?

Did it live up to the fantasies
that sustained you as you escaped
only by luck and position
those daily threats to your earthly life,
moles and snakes,
back hoes and cable trenchers
that would have untimely ripped you
from the larval womb?

And who told you to be so patient,
who promised that if you would just stay there,
content in the anonymity of clay,
you would one day shed your shell and,
glistening wet in a cloak of red and black and green,
rise in glory from the dust
to sing a love song the world had almost forgotten?

When at last you've answered those questions,
answer this one:
Which was better,
the solitude, the quiet life of patience and preparation,
or those final flights of ecstasy
within the community of lovers?

Something Like a Prayer

Ronald sleeps hotter than any boy I know
(a phrase he likes, as in
"You have more airplanes than any boy I know")
and scrunched into the twist of sheet and quilt
sweats everything wet within the first hour.
Every night I rearrange the covers,
straightening and flattening them
so he can breathe,
then sit on his bed
and press my face against his head,
wondering sometimes if his dreams
are filled like his life
with a million questions and no understanding,
and close my eyes into images of things
I want him to do,
ride a bike, catch a ball,
speak in regular boy tones,
sending my mind pictures
through his wet hair and into his dreams,
making this ritual something like a prayer
that one morning he will awaken
and live with me in this world.

Ghosts Send Messages by Freight Train
Adapted from Confessions of an
Accidental Businessman, *1996*

It was during that long wailing ambulance ride to Memphis
after the heart attack
she dreamed about her brothers,
killed those forty years ago
working on the railroad.
Not dreamed about them exactly
but about looking at their pictures,
studying their young and arrogant railroad man faces,
then noticing another picture frame,
empty and blank,
saved for her,
a sign it was not yet time for her to go.
So, she told me later,
she relaxed and enjoyed the trip.

Meanwhile trying to keep up with the ambulance
in my rental car
I heard the urgent whistle of a train
and looked to see it running parallel with the highway,
staying even with us.
Painted on the side of the freight cars
was some kind of slogan,
an advertising slogan I'm sure,
stretched along the train,
car after car,
saying simply
We're pulling for you
We're pulling for you
We're pulling for you

Taking Communion to the Shut-ins

It was a weekly duty of the elders
after regular church service in the sanctuary
to pack up the little boxes of bread
and the jugs of grape juice,
to get my list from the church office
and to visit the old and infirm,
aged and aging members who still lived at home,
and for whom the weekly Eucharist
had become so much a part of their lives
that to miss it one week would be to create
an unredeemable absence.

It was a simple routine, a greeting, a prayer,
the eating of the bread and drinking of the juice,
some parting pleasantries and on to the next one.
But it turned out not to be so easy
because of the stories and not just the stories
but how I became part of the stories,
an old fishing buddy, a son, a brother, a husband, a lost lover.
"You walk quick the way my husband used to walk;
my Daddy wondered why I would marry a man who walked so
quick."

I became not so much a messenger from the church
as a messenger from time and out of time,
resurrected for a few minutes into someone's main character,
changing from story to story
so at the end of the day I felt as if I had been found and lost,
celebrated and mourned,
over and over again,
yet helpless to be more that a witness
to the desperate attempt we all make

to understand the great mystery
of presence within absence.

Barb's Baby

We come to celebrate Christmas
but hear before the service
that a baby was born
with a collapsed lung and crossed arteries,
near death at birth,
and will require one of the new miracles
if he is to come into life
and walk among us,
if he is ever to light the altar candles
or squirm and giggle through a sermon
or play Joseph in the pageant
or sing in the youth choir,
if he is ever to fall in love
with a blond soprano
and try to sit next to her on the bus
on a spring tour to Washington,
if he is ever to leave home someday
and return only for Christmas,
to sit once again with his parents
and celebrate new life
in the place where now we pray
he will simply survive.

At the Autism Conference

A little boy named Nathan
sits on a chair
on a table
elevated so the teachers and parents and grad students
can see him do his trick.
A man with a foreign accent
and a beard
talks about eye contact
and prompts
and imitative verbalization
and reinforcers,
all the stuff the students are learning to do.
Nathan does what he does
and the students do what they do
and the people clap
and Nathan smiles.

Ghost Dance

by James A. Autry, Jr.

Don't despair the ruined lives,
the crosses to bear,
the churches burned down and smoking,
the rotted blood of hatred,
the civil wars,
crusades,
and inquisitions.
Hey, look who's in your back yard.
It's..........it's Jesus.
He's in everybody's back yard,
everybody's kitchen,
saying, "Look at me.
Get up.
Let's have some coffee.
I'll help you get through this day."

The Edge of Love

I lived too long on the edge of love,
making romance into love, making sex into love,
thinking I could discover the circumstances
in which love would reveal itself
like some Shangri-la
appearing out of the mists
after an arduous and desperate search.

But love waited for the inevitable,
showing itself at last in the unexpected terrain of loss,
waiting until grief exposed the unguarded me
to something I could not get or have or do,
could not see or hold, until I understood
that love is first about the possibilities of life
then about the certainty of loss
and finally about the exquisite pain of both.

Living with the Body

There are no rules for making peace with the body.
It's always trial and error, give and take,
on-the-job training.

This is not about diet and exercise,
this is about how hard it is
to make the body welcome in your life
instead of ignoring it
like an embarrassing relative in the back room.

For sixty years I have remembered the day
Mother jerked my face from her lap
because she felt the heat of my breath,
signaling to both of us,
I suppose,
that I could no longer be her baby boy.

Consider now the dilemma of Ronald
who struggled so hard to find his body in space,
learning finally to walk without falling,
who despite all the life science classes
and my straightforward explanations
still is confused and amused and sometimes alarmed
by his own erections.
What could be so concrete and yet so abstract?
And how could such a thing be explained
to a mind without even an understanding
of the age-old mechanics of the body
much less a way to imagine
the love, joy, and exhilaration of a union
that transcends the merely physical?

Then again, that's where we all struggle,
learning how to live peacefully within the body,
making it so welcome, so familiar, so intimate
that we no longer can tell
where the physical ends and the spiritual begins.

Learning to Pray

Ronald has heard people pray,
the ministers at church,
his grandfather at family gatherings,
me at the dinner table,
and he knows there's supposed to be something important
about those words and phrases,
but he doesn't get them right,
the prayers;
of course, he doesn't get a lot of things right.
"Grateful God," he says,
"Thank you for my ceiling fan
and my lawn mower and my cat . . ."

Once for no reason I could discern,
he stopped cutting the grass,
letting the mower engine die,
raised hands to face and said,
"You are a grateful God for giving me this Lawn Boy."
And in the Lord's Prayer he says,
"Hallowed be my name."

I used to think I should teach him to pray
the way everyone else does
but lately I don't know,
lately I find myself asking,
"How do I know that God is not
also to be grateful?"
Lately, I think less about God's majesty
and more about Ronald's struggle
to make sense of his place in this world,
never mind the next world.

Lately, I hear myself praying,
"Grateful God safely tucked away in Heaven,
we are thankful that Ronald
(hallowed be his name)
has come to live among us
in order that we may learn
how to face our disabilities,
how to find joy in ceiling fans and lawn mowers,
and how to pray."
Amen

From
Choosing Gratitude
(2012)

Summer

It is early.
I am driving northeast.
The sun skims the soybeans,
the corn rises from the ground
like a green wall at the end of the bean field
at an angle that's right in every way,
a comfort, an affirmation
of the dependability of things
good and growing.

Patience

The porch was alive with hummingbirds,
Swarming the feeders,
Hovering with their invisible wings,
Darting away and back,
Delighting all of us dude ranchers
Sitting in the big Adirondack chairs
After a day on the trail.
Ignoring the admonitions,
Ronald could not stay away.
"Don't worry," the ranch boss said,
"He can't catch them."
But the boss did not count on a patience
He'd never witnessed before:
A boy, moving as slowly as the wings were fast,
The birds waiting to be cupped in the boy's hands,
Then released back to their busy work.
Each christened with a new name.

Optimism

My grandmother seemed to live through the great depression
and world war two
with an attitude of expectation.
"When my ship comes in," she'd say,
"we'll buy that . . ." (whatever it was),
then go about her work with a cheerfulness
I could never understand.
What was the ship she was expecting,
and where was it coming from?
When I was older I decided she was just trying
to say we didn't have any money.
Later, I came to realize
that it was her way of saying
things will get better.
Later still, I understood
that it was her way to hold on to
the blessing of her eternal optimism.

A Sentimental Poem

For Sally on Our 20th Wedding Anniversary

I know that contemporary poets,
if they are to escape the wrath of critics,
must avoid the curse of sentimentality,
but here I am, twenty years married today,
with nothing to write about love
that is not sentimental:
a tumor, a surgery, a scribbled prayer
and the one hundred and thirty-ninth psalm;
the diagnosis of something wrong,
something wrong with our child;
hours and days and years
of working to help him find himself
in this world;
deaths of a father, a brother, a beloved sister,
more surgeries and recoveries,
a son in the struggle with addiction.
And I haven't even gotten to the joys,
not talked about the celebrations of life,
the friendships, the gatherings of family,
and the great and enduring spiritual quest.
If I am doomed to write of sentiment,
then let it be said that I also write of blessing,
all of it, the pain, fear, anguish,
laughter, whimsy, joy, blessings all,
because you arrived in my life
with an expectation of blessing,
a sure belief that there is nothing but abundance
and our job is to face it all with gratitude.

Every Day a Blessing
For Sally on Our 20th Wedding Anniversary

You have a way
of turning everything into a blessing,
of seeing the great mystery of goodness
in whatever happens,
in wherever we find ourselves in this life.

Waiting for the surgeons to cut your throat
you shared the 139th Psalm,
more to comfort me than you,
and somehow the surgery turned into
a celebration of life.

When they said something was wrong with our child,
and I sank into despair,
you learned what to do and how to do it,
showed the joy in every little triumph
from sign language to potty training,
and taught me the power of gratitude.

I've been told there is a light to guide us,
so bright it cannot be seen with the eyes,
that if we are to see it at all
we must find it inside ourselves.
Through all the fear and disappointment
and even through the loss of beloved people,
you have been able to live in that light,
and in turn have become the light
that I can see and follow,
the blessing of my life,
blessing upon blessing upon blessing.

From *Choosing Gratitude*

Disconnected

(Ten Years after the Death of My Brother)

How could I have explained
to the woman who answered
that I dialed not to reach her
but just to dial
that very number
as I have so many times before
to hear it ring once again
and remember for a moment
a voice I'll never hear again?

Ronald's Dance

Only he and I know that he is Gene Nelson
in Oklahoma; to everyone else
he is the strange kid dancing,
wild jerky arms swinging
spinning stomping jumping and twirling,
while the other dancers clap and laugh,
some with him some at him,
and I am seized by that terrible sense
of discovery and loss that accompanies
every new thing I see Ronald do.
Even now while in his mind everyone is celebrating
the exuberance and abandon of Gene Nelson
dancing on top of the railroad cars
I can't forget
that the train is pulling out of the station.

New Poems

Lost Dream

I have a recurring dream of taking a house
in a village in France in 1958
and going every morning
to a gathering of tables and chairs
outside a place with a Tabac sign,
then sitting with a rich coffee
in one of those little cups,
inhaling the aroma
before I take the first sip,
pretending to read the Herald Tribune
while men in their blue cotton work suits
pedal slowly, nodding a subtle greeting,
the stub of a Galloise
in the corner of their mouths,
and lifting my head to smell the
strangely aromatic and reassuring smoke,
nodding at women with baguettes
tucked under their armpits
and smiling to myself that perhaps the bread's flavor
might even be improved by that odiferous position.

When I'm awake I remember taking a house
in France a few years ago
and sitting at an outdoor café
and watching well-dressed men and women
rush by, faces buried in their cell phones,
stepping past street workers in jeans and t-shirts.
Women still went to the bakery for a baguette
and still tucked it carefully wrapped in paper
under their arms, then rushed to their cars.
Boisterous groups of young people
with cell phones and ear buds were everywhere.

And I realized that the France of my dream
no longer exists, but then,
neither does anywhere else.

Fighter Pilots

We knew how to fly
but we did not know how to live;
we knew how to perform the rituals of death,
but we did not know how to grieve;
we knew how to find laughter,
but we did not know how to find joy;
we knew how to do sex
but we did not know how to love;
we knew how to be romantic,
but we did not know how to be married;
we knew how to make babies,
but we did not know how to be parents.
In other words we were typical men
of our generation and damned proud of it.

Chaumont, France, October 1956

*(After getting a whiff of diesel fumes and wood smoke
during an October walk, 1997, Des Moines, Iowa)*

There are bicycles and workmen's denims and berets,
baguettes snugged into armpits,
tank scars on streets, rubble in vacant lots,
pock marks on buildings
from bullets of unknown nationality,
American names scratched into ancient walls.

In the cool damp morning
empty buckets wait by doorways,
and when the milkman fills them,
soot from coal and diesel exhaust
turns the white surface gray.

Inside the Hotel de France the maître d'
breaks an egg and whips mayonnaise for a ham sandwich,
then steps away leaving a young waiter to serve,
his short white jacket smudged at the sleeve
and his underarms smelling of cold water baths without soap.

On the air base villagers scour the grass
along the taxiways to shoot the big hares
that have made their own comeback
from the war days when they were the only meat.

In the fields farmers swing scythes,
and horses pull harvest wagons.

Everywhere, everything seems
as it always has been.

Paradise.

At the Air Force Reunion
Chaumont, France, July 4, 2006

A French woman is talking to me,
breath sour, teeth brown,
face fleshy, bosom heavy,
eyes sad, voice shaking,
"So hard for me this," she is saying,
and tells me about the love of her life,
gone these fifty years:
"I had his baby then he married a German girl,"
she says in a tone that makes me understand
that here the war is never really over.
She is crying silently.
"So hard for me this," she says.
"He was a pilot so tall so beautiful."

I am remembering the missions,
practice bombing runs on imaginary targets,
intense days of nuclear possibility,
drunken nights in the officers' club,
beer-drinking contests,
toasts to someone killed in an accident,
and of course the inevitable pilot talk
of sexual conquest.

She asks if I knew her pilot lover.
I say "No" yet I knew a dozen of him.
"I am looking for someone who knows him.
I want him to know he has a daughter,
and a grandson who is beautiful like him."

She asks then if she may hug me.

So here we are, two seventy-somethings,
hugging and crying together,
And I am thinking,
there's more than one kind of collateral damage.

In the Veterans Home

I am talking with an old man and a young man.
They are the same man.

The young man says, "I was the second soldier ashore in Africa.
The first guy went down but I passed him up."

The old man cries.

The young man continues,
"Bullets were flying and I had to keep moving."

The old man cries again.
A long silence.

The young man says, "I saw him later in the hospital
and he says, 'I know you, you're the guy who passed me up.'"

The old man sobs and wipes his eyes.

The young man continues,
"What could I do, Buddy? I had to keep moving.
And the guy says 'It's okay, I made it.'"

A long silence.
The old man wipes drool from his chin
with a tremoring yellowed handkerchief
and looks at me straight on.
"I never got no medals or anything,
but I've had a good life,"
then pressing the button on his electric scooter,
calls over his shoulder,
"Been good talking with you."

The Scar on My Hand

On my hand is a scar
made in anger fifty-three years ago
slamming a trailer window
that cracked my head as I walked
looking down at my little boy.

I do not remember the cut,
only Jimmy's face
looking up into the falling shards
of his father's violence.

At first I thought the blood was his
as he screamed at my hands
not shielding but dripping
onto his cheek and into his eye.

My injury was not serious
yet from time to time
the scar still flakes and peels
making me see Jimmy's terror again,
making me wonder how deeply he was pierced.

The Big Question Answered

I no longer struggle with the big question,
"Why are we here?"
I used to think the answer would be
something to do with ambition and work,
but finally realized
that I am here to father Ronald
so that he can do what he is here to do,
teach the other people.

Two Ronalds

There are two Ronalds now,
one dead and one alive,
and when I called little Ronald "Peckerduck,"
and old pet name from many lives ago
I thought of when big Ronald
hoisted me on his back,
his copy editor pencil piercing my knee
and me not caring
about the puncture which still shows
black through my skin,
the first copy editor's wound
and the only one that marked me forever.

The Paradox of Wanting and Needing
Aboard the Nile Pearl, March 31, 1990

Ronald has everything a six-year-old
could want except perhaps
certain kinds of cells in his brain.
That's the latest theory these days,
missing cells
that moderate things,
smells, sounds, movements, colors,
so that he can select
what he needs when he needs it,
and not be burdened
by what he does not need,
every signal from every sense,
so much that he tries to escape
and must be lured back
by the offerings of a father
who used to know
everything a six-year-old could want.

Clarity

Was it that Ronald died on the sixth
and we were married on the tenth
or that we were married on the sixth
and Ronald died on the tenth?
I have to think a moment to remember
that he waited until after the wedding
then came in a dream,
a curly haired blond child in a park
behind a transparent shield
through which I could see but not go
or even reach
except for one sleep-rousing kiss
in the instant of a telephone ringing.

Free Jazz Concert, Sanibel, 2014

In this ragged rendition
of Moonlight Serenade,
played with fading lips, unsure fingers,
who knows what memories
are aroused in this audience of gray faces:
close dancing perhaps in khaki uniforms,
big skirts, angora sweaters,
kisses, pledges of love, sad goodbyes,
evidenced now in this palm tree paradise
by nodding heads and tapping feet,
exchanges of knowing smiles,
a community of strangers transported
by this band of yesterday's musicians
passing through, as we all are, one last time.

On Seeing a Woman I Almost Remember Making Love With

New Orleans, November 20, 1998

Could it really have happened,
that I lay with this woman
in some French Quarter apartment,
the raw sounds of Bourbon Street
a background for her moans and screams
as I lay on my back and marveled
at how she rose and arched and plunged
until we both disappeared into ourselves?

Did she then smoke a cigarillo and sip brandy
fortifying herself for our next round,
or did we go out for raw oysters and gumbo
before we hit it again?

We are looking into each other's eyes.
We are searching for something not quite remembered,
something underneath the wrinkles and bleached hair.
And I shudder.

For Betty Sue on Reading Her Book

On the Concorde, N.Y.–Paris April 4, 1990

Myth maker and myth giver,
blesser of art and life and friendship,
quiet connection with the Goddesses,
I remember the first evening in Aspen,
when I thought
you were just another big-eyed,
honey-mouthed blonde from Texas,
and I thought I knew your story.
How could I have known
it was you who knew my story?

Marine Volunteers at the Autism Conference

Note: A group of marines from a local base volunteered for child-care duty at the conference.

The Leathernecks are here
doing the tough things.
When there's trouble
their only weapon is firm but gentle love,
a few good men
redefining what real heroes do.

Thinking of Two Friends Who Loved
One Another a Long Time Ago

We go our way never suspecting
who we might become (though some do
but always get it wrong).
We stop being the children we were,
and somewhere about then the die is cast
and nothing is ever the same,
but what there is becomes
with every day
more and more the same,
until we find ourselves thinking back
to how it seemed,
whether it ever was or not,
and wonder how we came to this,
different places, different times, different loves,
scattered like everyone else,
yet holding on to that ageless hope
for love still to come.

On Seeing a Painting of the Battle of Blenheim

A splendid duke on a splendid horse,
smiling at the coming victory,
his nobles and generals surrounding him
with confident satisfaction, gazing
toward the safely distanced battle, its
smoke obscuring the horizon.

This is art as propaganda
and we always seem to fall for it;
even I find myself entering the painting
as one of those guys with the duke,
yet in my heart I know the truth,
I know that my people are not on the horses,
but are out on the horizon,
under the smoke, shooting and hacking,
working endless horrors on one another,
bleeding into the history books
the duke's reputation as a great warrior.

What I'm Pretty Sure I Know

To shut up, to just keep quiet
when I think the world is waiting
for what I have to say about this or that;

To attend to my own grammar
and no else's;

To smile and say thank you
to the airport security people
whose job description requires
that they make it as difficult as possible
for the passengers;

To listen attentively to telephone menus;

And to ignore bad poems
including this one.

Love and Romance

Love is more important than romance,
I used to say,
and acceptance is more important than approval.
And people, especially women
who thought here at last might be the one,
would nod,
"yes that's true,"
and "We put too much emphasis on romance
in our culture,"
and "Acceptance, oh yes, acceptance
is the key," and so on.
But they didn't really believe it,
and as things turned out I was lying,
the cry of a romantic
desperate for approval.

Dilemma of the Real Poet

It seems to be a real poet
I must write a poem
that knows it is being written
and talks about it,
a kind of self-conscious poem,
a kind of poem in therapy,
asking "Where did I come from
and who shaped me along the way
and where am I to go now?"

How does the real poet answer such a poem?
There is the psychoanalytical response:
"Tell me, poem, how does this make you feel,
this knowing that you are being written
even as we speak?"

Or the New Age response:
"You, poem, are okay as you are;
live in the nowness and not the wasness
or even the to-beness,
Tune in to the universal unconscious
from which you come and are going."

Or perhaps the new proud American response:
"Shape up, wimpy poem, get back to the old values
that made this country's poems great.
Give up this decadent, secular humanist whining.
Start rhyming, get metrical.
Then you'll be proud and stand tall again."

But who am I kidding?
Myself perhaps but not the poem.

I know that it, like my friends or children,
having told me the problem and asked me the questions,
would just listen politely
then go ahead and be written
as if I had said nothing at all.

Traveling Dreams

They say dreams tell the tale,
truth revealed in strange messages
when wheels hitting the runway
jerk me awake between somewhere and somewhere,
or twisting in a hotel bed
a beat before the alarm,
then preoccupied with waking
and unable to remember,
to find the message,
but feeling most often a darkness,
a foreboding,
thinking that I don't need the subconscious
to remind me we are dying,
wondering when do I dream those other truths,
the ones worth going to sleep for.

Strategic Planning Advice

Here in the midst
of your planning and forecasting,
your future scenarios and contingencies,
consider this day.
This day, now, awaits your best work.

A Cliché Poem

If you live long enough,
everything becomes a cliché,
whatever you attempt
before you are able to finish it,
becomes a cliché,
so whatever it was going to be
just lies there waiting to be finished,
yet another cliché.

Your conversations on subjects,
no matter how profound
you once thought they could be,
begin to dissolve into a morass
of redundancy, the very definition of cliché.

You even get tired of shaving your cliché of a face.

Parkinson's

My life has been around a while
but, I can tell, is thinking about
moving on and taking me along.
I'd rather stay but know
I don't have a choice.
All I can do is drag my feet
finding reason after reason not to go.

CPSIA information can be obtained at www.ICGtesting.com
Printed in the USA
LVOW06s0158100715

445622LV00033B/1073/P